W9-BND-150

APR 10 '85	DATE		
MAR 0 2 1987			
" JAN 13 '90			
SEP 2 9 1994			

FAITH
OF OUR
FATHERS

VOLUME TWO

Reform and Renewal

John Patrick Donnelly, S.J.

A Consortium Book

To My Mother with Gratitude for Her Many Sacrifices

Preface

For the basic outline of the book I must thank Thomas Pearl, the editor of *Faith of Our Fathers*. Dr. Keith Egan of Marquette University's theology department gave me valued suggestions for improving the treatment of the medieval church and the Catholic reformation. The chapters on the reformation profited from the advice of Dr. Robert Kolb, Director of the Center for Reformation Research, St. Louis, and the Rev. Robert Bireley of Loyola University, Chicago. Specialized help came from Dr. James Lee and Dr. John Berens of Marquette's history department.

John Patrick Donnelly, S.J.
Marquette University, Milwaukee
December 15, 1976

Table of Contents

1

After The Dark Ages

The Rise of the Barbarian Kingdoms

In 410 the Visigoths sacked Rome, then devastated southern Gaul before settling in Spain. Other Germanic tribes stripped province after province from the shattered Roman Empire in the West. The Vandals set up a kingdom in North Africa, and the Burgundians took over much of Gaul, while the Angles and the Saxons carved up England. The Romanized natives were too civilized and too cowed to resist effectively the awesome invaders. Relations between the conquered Roman Christians and the barbarians were uneasy, for they differed in language, law, and culture; above all they differed in religion since most of the barbarians were Arians, Christians who denied Christ's full divinity.

The Franks were the great exception. Clovis, their energetic and unscrupulous king, was convinced that the Christian God had helped his armies and together with his warriors accepted baptism from Catholic bishops. The religious unity of the Franks with their Gallo-Roman subjects gave their state a solidarity not possessed by the other barbarian kingdoms, so that it soon expanded over France, Belgium and much of Germany. The Frankish rulers forged close relations with the popes. They aided the papal legate, St. Boniface, in reforming the unruly, immoral, and superstitious Frankish church and encouraged his missionary efforts in Germany.

3

They also protected the papacy from the encroaching Lombards. In turn the papacy gave its blessing to the Frankish rulers, especially Pepin the Short.

Charlemagne: The New Constantine

Pepin's son, known as Charles the Great or Charlemagne (768-814), changed the direction of history more than any other medieval ruler. Charlemagne, who united most of western Europe under his rule, was largely responsible for shifting the center of medieval civilization from the Mediterranean to the northern lands between the Loire and the Elbe; he began German domination over Italy and the German drive toward the east; and he helped revive the classical tradition in medieval culture.

Even Charlemagne's physical appearance was larger than life. His friend Einhard describes him thus: "The Emperor was strong and well built. He was tall in stature...and his eyes were large and penetrating. His nose was a bit longer than usual, and he had a full head of white hair while his expression was open and joyous. Hence he always appeared dignified and masterful whether seated or standing." Late in life the emperor suffered from gout much aggravated by too much roast meat. His sexual appetites were equally large.

From the first Charlemagne pursued an aggressive foreign policy in which religious zeal played a part. He used the encroachments of the Lombard king to invade Italy and assume the Lombard crown for himself in 774. His war against the pagan Saxons in northern Germany involved campaigns nearly every year from 772 to 804. Charlemagne offered the Saxons a simple alternative: baptism or death. Most chose baptism but repeatedly revolted and slew the missionaries that Charlemagne had planted among them. The emperor finally broke their resistance by mass deportations to other areas and by bringing in Frankish settlers. His conquest of the Avar robber state opened the upper Danube to Germanic colonization. To stop Moslem raids from Spain Charlemagne conducted several campaigns south of the Pyrenees and set up a Spanish province of his empire. From here and from the independent Christian pockets in the north the Christians began their seven hundred year reconquest of Spain from the Moslems.

No Christian ruler since Constantine and Justinian had wielded such power. The half-remembered traditions of Roman imperial rule, the widespread feeling that there should be a secular counterpart to the spiritual rule of the pope, and Charlemagne's own accomplishments lay behind the drama in St. Peter's basilica on Christmas day, 800. As Pope Leo III placed the diadem of the Caesars on the head of Charlemagne, the people proclaimed, "Life and victory to Charles Augustus, great and pacific emperor, crowned by God." That event launched the Holy Roman Empire on a thousand years of weal and woe. Leo probably desired little more than Charlemagne's support against local enemies, but later popes found in the coronation a claim for papal supremacy over the emperors.

Certainly Charlemagne recognized no such supremacy. He saw himself as both successor of the Caesars and the new David called by God to sacral kingship. While he acknowledged the spiritual authority of the pope, he insisted on controlling the church as tightly as he did the state. In 796 he wrote Leo III: "It is our task with God's help to defend everywhere the holy church outwardly by armed might from the attacks of pagans and the ravages of infidels and to strengthen it inwardly by the knowledge of the Catholic faith. It is your duty, holy father, to aid our army with uplifted hands like Moses so that by your help the Christian people under God's guidance and gift may everywhere and always attain victory..." In Charlemagne's scheme the pope was hardly more than an imperial chaplain who prayed for the church while the emperor ruled and protected it.

Charlemagne's practice fitted his theory. He appointed all the bishops in his realm and organized them into metropolitan provinces under archbishops. Churchmen occupied most of the important posts in the imperial chancery, and bishops shared with the counts the administration of the three hundred counties of the Empire. Charlemagne usually entrusted the most important tasks of his *missi dominici*, or travelling inspectors, to bishops and abbots since they were his best educated subjects. Even liturgical and dogmatic questions did not escape Charlemagne's control. For a century the papacy had helped the monks of the Byzantine Empire in their struggle for the veneration of sacred images against iconoclastic emperors. The second council of Nicea of 787 finally upheld the Roman view in the east, but to the pope's discomfort Charlemagne steered through a synod at Frankfort in 794 a decree on images which fell far short of the Roman view.

Charlemagne tried to foster learning and literature, but the age merits the title of Carolingian Renaissance only by comparison with the abysmal ignorance of the previous centuries. Charlemagne himself could speak several languages but never learned to write and could barely read. The age created little original but did pass on many manuscripts in the firm Carolingian minuscule hand which provides the basis of the type used in all western European languages today.

Charlemagne's empire was the product of his genius and did not long survive him. His son Louis the Pious lacked talent as a ruler and followed the disastrous Frankish custom of dividing the empire as if it were a private estate among his three sons, who soon fell to fighting one another. In fact the empire had little to unite it except a common religion. The people spoke primitive forms of German, French, Italian and Spanish. The economy was largely restricted to production for local consumption. The break-up of the empire was speeded by Magyar horsemen from Hungary, Moslem raiders from Africa and especially by the pagan Norsemen who drove their dragonships far up the rivers and then plundered far and wide.

Monasticism and the Preservation of the Past

Monasticism existed before Christianity among Buddhists and Jewish Essenes, but Christian monasticism arose as an independent response to certain biblical passages and to specific conditions in Egypt in the late third century. St. Paul praised the life of dedicated celibacy (1 Cor. 7) and Christ urged the rich young man to sell all, give the proceeds to the poor and follow him (Luke 18:22). The early Christian ideal had been the martyr, but as martyrdom became rare and crowds of halfhearted Christians flooded the church in the wake of Constantine's conversion, many zealous Christians felt called to a more rigorous life of prayer and renunciation. Egypt, with its mild climate and oppressive taxation, had a tradition of *anachoresis* or taking to the desert.

St. Antony (251-356), the first anchorite or hermit, spiritualized this tradition. He devoted himself to prayer and simple manual work; sometimes he was subject to severe depression and temptation but he persevered in his calling. His temptations later became a favorite subject of Renaissance art, especially for Bosch and Brueghel, who picture the saint attacked by grotesque devils. Twice only Antony left the desert and visited Alexandria, once to encourage the faithful in the persecution of Diocletian and once to support the bishop against the Arians. As his fame spread, Egyptians flocked out to ask advice or become his disciples. St. Athanasius, the patriarch of Alexandria, wrote a biography of Antony whose challenging effect on readers is described in St. Augustine's *Confessions.*

Hundreds and then thousands took to the Egyptian desert as hermits in quest of holiness. Gradually a need for a more structured life became evident. Younger monks needed guidance and the sick and old needed care. A community could answer these needs and direct rampant individualism and asceticism into safer channels. In 323 St. Pachomius founded the first monastic community and gave it a rule noted for moderation. Seventeen years later his sister Mary gathered the first community of nuns.

Within a few decades monasticism arose in Palestine and Syria. The first monastery in Constantinople dates from 382. The great monastic legislator for the Greek church was St. Basil. His rule, which still inspires Orthodox monasticism, is not a juridical constitution in the western sense but spiritual counsel which stresses living in community as the framework for spiritual growth. Although Basil emphasizes obedience, the abbot in the east has seldom had as much power as in the west, whereas the individual monk has had more freedom.

Western monasticism began in the late fourth century. St. Athanasius spread the monastic ideal during his years of exile in the west. More important were the writings of St. Jerome, who returned to Rome after several years as a monk in Syria; when he returned to the east, several great Roman ladies accompanied him to become nuns. St. Augustine organized his priests at Hippo into a semi-monastic community; his guidance for them and his writings on virginity did much to encourage monasticism. Even earlier St. Martin had established a similar community of priests near Tours. No less influential was John Cassian who spent from 385 to 400 as a monk in Egypt before founding two monasteries at Marseilles. He distilled the sayings and experiences of the Egyptian monks into his *Conferences*, which became required reading in monasteries for over a thousand years.

The greatest early flowering of western monasticism came in distant Ireland during the fifth and sixth centuries. Indeed, the church organization in Ireland was more monastic than episcopal; monks with episcopal ordination continued to live under the jurisdiction of their abbots. Sometimes the abbots themselves were bishops. Often monasticism intermeshed with the clan structure of Irish society, the clan leaders serving as abbots for two thousand or more monk-clansmen. Irish monks rivalled the Egyptians in their pursuit of physical austerities, but their love for learning and gift for poetry and art are not found in Egypt.

The Roman senator Flavius Magnus Aurelius Cassiodorus fostered a more genteel monasticism at the Vivarium, his villa at the toe of Italy. The long life of Cassiodorus (c. 485-580) reflected the gradual decline of late antiquity into barbarism. After an excellent classical education he spent his middle years as a high administrator in the service of the Ostrogothic kings of Italy. When their rule crumpled, he devoted several years to studying theology and then retired to the Vivarium. Never a monk himself, he remained the patron and advisor of the monks. Much of their day passed in prayer, but the special contribution of the monks at the Vivarium was the preservation of learning in a barbaric world. Cassiodorus saw this as a cultural and religious duty: "Happy is the aim, praiseworthy the eagerness, to reveal tongues with the fingers, silently to give salvation to men, to fight with pen and ink against the attacks of the devil. Satan receives a wound in every word written by him who makes fresh texts of the ancient law of the Lord."

Cassiodorus was himself a prolific author. He wrote a history of the Goths and of the early church, scripture commentaries, and twelve books of correspondence. More interesting is the book he wrote to show his monks how to copy manuscripts and avoid copying errors. His greatest work, *The Fundamentals of Divine and Human Readings*, outlines a program of studies for his monks in both religious and secular subjects. The Vivarium did not long survive its founder, but later Benedictine monasteries took up the work of copying the treasures of antiquity. The monks most prized the Bible and the writings of the church fathers, but it is due to their efforts that much of classical Latin literature and ancient science has survived.

The life of St. Benedict (c. 480-543), the great legislator of western monasticism, remains shadowy despite a colorful biography by Pope Gregory the Great. Like most medieval hagiographers, the good pope seldom hesitated when choosing between the accurate and the marvelous. Benedict certainly founded a small monastery at Monte Cassino between

Rome and Naples and gave posterity the finished rule which became basic for western monasticism. Although short, his rule gives practical and flexible directions for all aspects of monastic life and combines high spirituality with a physical moderation which stresses charity, harmony and family spirit over the austerity, rivalry and individualism so noteworthy in Celtic monasticism. In France alone there were twenty rules in operation around 600; some two centuries later the Benedictine rule had replaced nearly all other rules throughout western Europe. The endorsement of popes, Charlemagne and Louis the Pious hastened its spread, but its triumph depended primarily on its own merits.

What was Benedictine life like? Obviously it varied enormously during the period 600 to 1150 when monasticism was central to European civilization. The early monasteries were really an enlarged family. Cluny at its height had three hundred monks and was a small city. Still medieval monastic life had a basic rhythm in spite of local and seasonal variations. A typical day might run thus: rise at 2:00 AM to sing Matins and Lauds in chapel until 4:00. Prime was sung at 6:00, with Terce, Sext, and None following at three hour intervals, each taking some fifteen minutes. There was no breakfast, but a solid meal at noon and at 6:00 PM. There would be a siesta after lunch in the summer. Manual work would occupy several hours in mid-morning and mid-afternoon. There would also be two hours for reading and reflection in the morning. Vespers was often sung just before supper, which was followed by Compline. The monk went to bed shortly after sunset, as did most men in the pre-electric age. In early Benedictine monasticism when most monks were not ordained, daily mass was not usual although there might be communion. By the eleventh century many monks were priests who celebrated mass daily and also attended the abbot's mass. The increasing length and splendor of liturgical services gradually cut down or completely crowded out manual labor.

The history of monasticism, like the life of the Christian and of the church itself, centers on reform efforts after periods of decay. One reform centered on the Burgundian abbey of Cluny where five long-lived abbots ruled in sequence for nearly all the years from 927 to 1157. Cluny's fame as a spiritual powerhouse caused other monasteries to seek affiliation. Monks in the daughter houses took vows of obedience to the abbot of Cluny, who appointed a prior as superior. To insure that the seventy daughter houses followed Cluny's customs and reforms, the abbot spent much of his time visiting them. The Cluniac reform had weaknesses. It was limited by the energy of the head abbot. Cluny produced little literature or theology, although it turned out brilliant illuminated manuscripts and celebrated the liturgy with a magnificence unmatched before or since.

Cluniac observance was splendid, but was it the ideal of St. Benedict? Many reformers thought not and sought to return to a more simple and pristine monasticism. Several tried to combine communal living with the life-style of the old hermits. The Camaldolese and Vallombrosans did this in Italy; more successful still were the Carthusians who had 190 houses noted for their fervor all over Europe. But it was the founders of the Cistercian abbey of Citeaux who were most influential in revivifying the Benedictine ideal. After St. Bernard became the dynamic abbot of Clairvaux, Cistercian observance spread so widely that by the late middle ages there were seven hundred Cistercian monasteries, plus nine hundred convents for nuns. The Cistercians insisted on a literal application of the Benedictine rule, thereby cutting down the forest of minor offices, litanies and processions that had grown up since St. Benedict. This also allowed time for manual work. They tried to minimize involvement in feudalism by locating their houses in the rugged waste areas that still occupied much of Europe. Many of their members were lay brothers from the lower classes whose Herculean labors turned hills and forests into some of Europe's finest farms, vineyards and sheepruns. Freed from the conventions of medieval farming, the Cistercian brothers became the agricultural pioneers of the age. Perhaps they were too successful, for they created the wealth and its attendant problems that they were seeking to avoid. Originally each Benedictine monastery was completely autonomous; hence there was no Benedictine order, only a rule and hundreds of monasteries that followed it. In contrast, the Cistercian abbots met annually at Citeaux to legislate for the whole order, thereby insuring an unprecedented uniformity.

St. Anselm

From the seventh to the twelfth century the vast majority of literate men were educated in monastic schools since only the monasteries had the continuity, dedication, libraries and scholars to provide effective education. These schools subordinated secular learning, chiefly literature and logic, to theology. Even theology took on a monastic coloration. The philosophical theology and systematic rigor of thirteenth century scholasticism was foreign to monastic inclinations. Monastic theology was pastoral, not in the sense that the monks applied theology to the needs of lay Christians; rather they adapted it to their own needs and spiritual experiences. Monastic theology was based on scripture and the church fathers, especially St. Augustine, but it always looked to the monk's own inward experience of union with God. Where the scholastic theologian tried to know God, the monk sought to experience Him.

The greatest Benedictine theologian and the most powerful Christian thinker between Augustine and Aquinas was St. Anselm (1033-1109), who both summed up and transcended the thought of the monastic schools. His life suggests how cosmopolitan the medieval church could be on its higher levels. Anselm was an Italian from Piedmont who studied in France, entered the Norman monastery of Bec, and having served as prior and abbot, became Archbishop of Canterbury in 1093. Although his biographers emphasize his affability and gentleness, Anselm defended church freedom and papal rights so vigorously that the English kings William Rufus and Henry I exiled him.

But it is Anselm the thinker rather than Anselm the churchman who compels attention even today. He was deeply indebted to the writings of St. Augustine both for content and style and disclaimed any wish to go beyond his master, but his daring application of dialectic to the mysteries of faith broke new ground. Since he antedated the later scholastic distinctions between the areas proper to philosophy and theology, from later perspectives he has appeared at once a fideist and a rationalist. All his thinking was dominated by a single principle, "I believe so that I can understand"—he began from faith and then used reason to reach a deeper understanding of the content of his faith. Reason does not attain faith as the last conclusion in a series of arguments, nor does it remove the mystery of faith.

In his *Monologium*, Anselm gave three proofs for the existence of God which argued from the empirical existence of degrees of created goodness to the existence of an absolute Good. Anselm long searched for a self-contained proof that would depend solely on the principle of contradiction without appealing to any empirical evidence. His *Proslogion* gives his proof: "We indeed believe that You are the being than which no greater can be conceived. Even the fool (of Psalm 14:1) who denies God is forced to agree that the being than which no greater can be conceived exists at least in the mind; for when he hears the expression, he understands its meaning, and whatever is understood exists in the mind. And certainly the being than which no greater can be conceived cannot exist in the mind alone. For if it is in the mind alone, it can be conceived as existing also in reality, which is something greater. Therefore if the being than which no greater can be conceived exists in the mind alone, something greater can be conceived. But this cannot be. Therefore the being than which no greater can be conceived exists both in the mind and in reality."

Perhaps no equally short passage in the history of philosophy has stirred so much discussion. Gaunilo, a monk from nearby Marmoutier, replied that the argument jumps from the conceptual to the real order: now just because one can conceive of the Blessed Isles as a perfect land, it does not follow that they exist. Anselm replied to Gaunilo, and the argument has gone on ever since. Aquinas, Locke and Kant sided with Gaunilo, whereas Bonaventure, Descartes and Hegel have taken up and elaborated Anselm's case.

Anselm also applied his dialectic powers in his *Why the God-Man?*, which tried to give reasons for Christ's incarnation and death. By sin man has offended the infinite God, hence the need either for man's punishment or satisfaction to God. Sinful man cannot make adequate satisfaction. Granted that God wills man's salvation, only Christ the God-man can make satisfaction because as man he can act on behalf of men and as God his free acceptance of death earns a satisfaction that has infinite merit. Anselm's argument not only profoundly influenced medieval thought but also undergirded the theology of Luther and Calvin concerning Christ and salvation.

2

The Age of Faith

The Crusades
The two centuries following the death of Charlemagne and the breakup of his empire cast Europe once more into a dark age, but it was the darkness of a womb pregnant with promise. The promise appeared with the renaissance of the twelfth century and the mature civilization of the thirteenth. Several factors contributed to this growth. Improved agricultural techniques were crucial. Better plows of iron cut into the heavy soil of northern Europe. Horses with efficient collars gradually replaced oxen as draught animals, while better use of manure and the introduction of a three field system of crop rotation to replace the two field system brought higher yields. More food meant that Europe could sustain more people; in England, for example, population rose from 1,100,000 in 1086 to 3,700,000 in 1346. The revival of commerce together with the population increase stimulated the growth of towns. Medicine and hygiene remained primitive, so that life expectancy stayed under thirty even though the twelfth and thirteenth centuries were not notable for great plagues. The dominance of young men, who hurried to make their mark before being crowded off the stage of life, gave medieval civilization much of its vibrance, violence and peculiar melancholy. Perhaps nothing illustrates this burgeoning, zesty, yet deeply religious civilization better than the crusades.

For centuries Christianity had been on the defensive against Islam. Arab armies conquered nearly half of the Christian world within a century after the death of Mohammed. Syria and Egypt, lands rich in Christian history, came under Moslem control almost immediately, even though most of the population long remained Christian; indeed, these countries still contain considerable minorities of Maronite and Coptic Christians. The conquest of Persia and North Africa was followed by the invasion of Spain in 711. The Arabs invested Constantinople by land and sea in 673-677 and again in 717 but were unable to capture the city; their failure enabled the Byzantines to rule Asia Minor and the Balkans for centuries to come. Aside from the conquest of Sicily, the western expansion of Islam stopped after the Franks defeated them at Tours in central France in 732, exactly a century after the death of the Prophet.

Moslem expansion ceased not because of Christian strength but because Moslem zeal waned and the Arabs broke into hostile factions and sects. Even so Moslem culture achieved a golden age during the ninth century under the Abbasid caliphs of Baghdad. The conversion of the Seljuk Turks and their conquest of Baghdad, Persia, and Syria meant that Islam was again advancing. At Manzikert in 1071 the Turks inflicted a crushing blow on the Byzantines and overran most of Asia Minor. The new Byzantine emperor Alexis I turned to the West for support.

Urban II was sympathetic and called for a crusade at the Council of Clermont in 1095. Even the pope must have been surprised by the mighty shout "God wills it" that answered his sermon. Thousands of knights donned the red-crossed tunic of the crusade and prepared to risk their lives against the infidel. What motivated this unique enthusiasm? Undoubtedly Urban himself saw the crusade as an opportunity to heal the schism between eastern and western churches and enhance papal prestige. Probably he foresaw that the crusade would turn the swords of turbulent nobles from mutual slaughter to a "better" use. Few medieval Christians doubted that God's will sanctioned the use of military might against infidels, nor did their Moslem opponents. Religious zeal, however misdirected, was doubtless the chief motive of the early crusaders. Moreover, the feudal aristocracy was trained to arms—fighting for God's cause had an instant appeal that prayer and penance could never match, especially since the pope promised a full indulgence for the sins of crusaders. Pilgrimages to Compostella, Rome and Jerusalem had enormous prestige; an armed pilgrimage to rescue the places sanctified by Christ's life and death had a unique appeal to medieval religious psychology. There were also secular motives: why not exchange the routine of castle and manor for travel, adventure and glory? Especially for younger sons of the nobility the crusade gave hope of a better life, perhaps an estate in one of the crusader kingdoms.

Accordingly thirty thousand Christians trekked into Syria on the first crusade. They found the Seljuk Turks divided, captured Jerusalem in 1099, and set up four mutually jealous crusader states. It was the Moslem reconquest of the County of Edessa, the most exposed crusader state, that sparked the second crusade, which accomplished little and was disgraced by pogroms against the German Jews. Meanwhile the constant need for reinforcements led to the formation of military religious orders such as the Templars and the Hospitalers. The capture of Jerusalem by Saladin in 1187 precipitated the third crusade. The nobility of Saladin and the clashing personalities of the Christian leaders, Frederick Barbarossa, Philip Augustus, and Richard the Lion-Hearted, have given the third crusade an epic luster not matched by its accomplishments. The Christians retained a strip of land along the seacoast and the right to visit Jerusalem; more lasting was the conquest of Cyprus, which remained a western outpost until the Turks captured it from the Venetians in 1571.

The fourth crusade was a momument of moral bankruptcy. The dissolution of Saladin's empire inspired the greatest medieval pope, Innocent III, to call for renewed effort. When the crusaders who had gathered at Venice carried out the Doge's suggestion that they capture Venice's Dalmatian rival Zara as the price of their voyage, Innocent excommunicated the whole crusade. Meanwhile the crusaders had sailed to Constantinople to restore the ousted emperor Isaac. This they did, but when the city rose against him, the crusaders sacked the city, then elected one of their leaders emperor and carved up the empire into feudal principalities. The Latin empire so erected lasted from 1204 to 1261 when the Byzantines managed to recover Constantinople; but their empire never fully recovered, and the sack embittered relations between Rome and the eastern Orthodox for centuries.

Four further crusades from 1218 to 1270 lack historical importance, although Jerusalem was briefly restored to Christian rule. In contrast, crusades within Europe itself became increasingly important. Crusaders played a vital role in Spain, particularly at the battle of Las Navas de Tolosa in 1212, which brought most of southern Spain under Christian rule. Three great crusading orders were founded in Spain and eventually passed under royal control. On the south coast of the Baltic the Teutonic Knights gradually conquered the pagan Prussians and Estonians, began their Christianization and spread German colonists from Danzig to Riga. Nor did the papacy hesitate to turn crusaders against heresy, successfully against the Cathari, less so against the Hussites. On occasion the popes even called for crusades against political opponents such as emperor Frederick II, but these operations were sham crusades. In the fifteenth century the popes repeatedly proclaimed crusades against the Ottoman Turks who were advancing up the Balkans; these crusades were either ignored by Europe or defeated by the Turks. On the balance, the crusades were a failure; they did not attain their goal of freeing Jerusalem, nor were they so important for stimulating trade or fostering the exchange of ideas between east and west as historians once thought.

The Crisis of Medieval Thought

Far more than the crusades, the rise of the universities testifies to the dynamism of medieval Europe. Not only are many medieval universities still functioning, but all the universities of the world today consciously imitate a tradition which goes back to Paris and Bologna in the twelfth century. Still the medieval university had striking differences from its modern descendants; it possessed no libraries, no laboratories, indeed, no buildings at all; much less were there organized extra-curriculars such as athletics, dramatics or school newspapers.

In medieval Latin *universitas* could mean any association of men, for instance a guild. In fact the universities were essentially guilds made up of apprentices (undergraduates), journeymen (bachelors of arts), and masters (professors with a master's degree). Most universities followed the Paris pattern and were guilds of masters; but several followed Bologna, which specialized in law and had older students, and were essentially associations of students who made regulations and hired professors.

Obviously the universities were associations for internal self-regulation but they were also organized for protection from businessmen and the local citizens. Several thousand students supplied much extra business for the medieval town; students and professors had to rent lodging and buy food in the local marketplace. They also did a great deal of beer drinking in the local taverns; indeed student drinking songs, often parodies on Latin hymns, are good examples of medieval humor. Student high spirits often led to friction with the townsmen, sometimes to full scale riots. So many of the students were clerics that students in general came to share clerical immunity from regular police and court jurisdiction, much to the annoyance of ordinary townsmen. Rowdy behavior was partly checked by the formation of colleges, which were originally supervised residence halls for students and only later began to offer lectures. Should hostility to students or price gouging become excessive, the university could threaten its ultimate weapon against the townspeople: simply moving the university to another town. Since the university only rented halls and lodging, using nearby churches for major gatherings, the threat to move was plausible. Usually merchants who faced disaster forced the town government to knuckle under to student demands, but in several instances actual transfers took place and gave rise to new universities.

Paris, whose eight thousand students made it the largest medieval university, evolved from a cathedral school famous for teachers such as the stormy Peter Abelard. Many other distinguished cathedral schools of the twelfth century, Chartres for instance, never developed into universities. Paris had the advantage of the largest population in northern Europe in the thirteenth century (perhaps 80,000 inhabitants), and since it was the seat of the royal government, its commune had only limited authority. Moreover the king and the pope showered the university with charters and privileges. Indeed, most of the eighty universities of the later middle ages were princely foundations. No doubt princes and popes wished to patronize learning, but they also had a pragmatic need for trained manpower, which then as now the universities were uniquely able to supply. Increasingly university training became almost a prerequisite for advancement in both church and state except for noblemen.

Books were few at the medieval university; students could rent some but were expected to compile their own book from the professors' lectures. Lectures usually took the form of commentaries on the established works in each discipline— Galen in medicine, Justinian's code in civil law, Gratian's *Decretals* in canon law, Aristotle for philosophy, and the Bible and Peter Lombard's *Sentences* for theology. Disputations supplemented the lectures, usually on subject matter assigned beforehand, but twice annually the masters engaged in quodlibet disputations in which they took on all comers on any subject. The professor's task was demanding and his training long. At thirteenth-century Paris the Master of Arts degree took four years after the Bachelor's. Civil lawyers studied eight years and masters in theology twelve beyond the arts degree.

In the cathedral schools of the early twelfth century education centered on the traditional seven liberal arts: grammar, logic, rhetoric, arithmetic, geometry, astronomy and music (really musical theory). By mid-century logic overshadowed grammar and literature. Aristotle's logical works had been available in Latin translation ever since the collapse of the Roman world, but most of his scientific and philosophical works were unknown in the West until the second half of the twelfth century. Gradually Latin translations, first from Arabic versions through Spain, then directly from the Greek, began circulating in the universities. Suddenly the Christian West faced the whole heritage of the widest ranging intellect of the ancient world. Aristotle contributed to both science and philosophy his unique gift for precise definition and systematic classification. Despite rearguard condemnations by conservative churchmen, Aristotelian philosophy soon dominated the undergraduate curriculum.

The conservative distrust of Aristotle was not entirely without foundation. Aristotle was a pagan, and if his thought contained resources Christian theology could exploit, it also seemed to shut the God of the Bible into a self-contained system of necessary natural laws. Aristotle seemed hostile to personal immortality and seemed to teach the necessary existence of the world from all eternity, which contradicted the Christian teaching that God freely created the world in time. Digesting Aristotle together with his Greek and Arab commentators presented an enormous challenge to the thirteenth century.

The Middle Ages can be called the age of faith only with reservations. For the mass of peasants religion was a confused mixture of Christianity and pagan residues. There were

university agnostics at medieval Paris and Padua just as at
Berkeley and Cambridge today. The spread of Aristotle precipitated a crisis of faith that took various forms. Siger of
Brabant (c. 1235-1281), professor of philosophy at Paris, illustrates Latin Averroïsm which overwhelmingly accepted
Aristotle as interpreted by the Arab Averroës as philosoph-
ically true. What of those points on which Aristotle and
Averroës seemed to contradict the teaching of faith? Here
Siger suggested that even though Aristotle teaches the
necessary conclusions of reason, the Christian must bow to
the higher truth of faith. There is no evidence to doubt Siger's
sincerity—Dante gives him a high place in the *Paradiso*—but
other Latin Averroïsts undoubtedly jettisoned faith in favor
of Aristotle.

St. Thomas Aquinas (c. 1225-1274), an Italian Dominican
who taught at Paris and in Italy, took up the challenge of
pagan philosophy. He saw that most of Aristotelian philosophy could be used to buttress Christian faith, especially if
freed from the Arab accretions that sharpened its determin-
istic aspects. Accordingly Aquinas wrote many commentaries on Aristotle which interpreted him in a Christian sense.
He did not hesitate to supplement Aristotle with his own in-
sights and ideas deriving from Plato. Not only does the
Summa Theologiae, the masterwork of Aquinas, incorporate
many Aristotelian concepts, but its whole program of
synthetic theology recalls Aristotle's scientific method and
outlook. Unlike Siger, St. Thomas refused to admit that the
necessary conclusions of right reason can ever oppose Christian faith. Just as grace perfects nature, so revelation supple-
ments reason. Revelation provides a guide which can help
correct the mistakes of Aristotle. The Christian thinker can
prove many points which uneducated believers accept on
faith; in other areas reason gives deeper insight into the
meaning of faith and furnishes arguments to defend it. Despite his confidence in reason, Aquinas held that Christians
cannot explain rationally but must accept on the authority

of God's revelation such deep mysteries as the incarnation, the Trinity and the eucharist.

Neither Siger nor Aquinas represented the mainstream of medieval Christian thought. Most theologians belonged to a diffuse Augustinian-Franciscan school which took a cautious stance toward Aristotle. Their first great representative was St. Bonaventure (1221-1274), whose early career at Paris closely parallels that of St. Thomas. At thirty-six Bonaventure was elected general of the Franciscans and guided them skillfully during a stormy period, but his administrative duties cut into his output as a theologian. Together with all scholastic theologians he made use of Aristotelian concepts but his basic outlook came from St. Augustine and centered on God and the soul, or more precisely on the mind's journey through the stages of philosophy, faith, theology and contemplation up to ecstatic union with God. Bonaventure rejected the autonomous role that Siger and Aquinas gave reason, voicing his alarm in his *Conference on the Six Days of Creation*, which he gave at Paris in 1273.

The bishop of Paris, Etienne Tempier, shared Bonaventure's fears; as early as 1270 he had condemned thirteen philosophical propositions which dealt with the human soul, free will, and providence as taught by the secular Aristotelians. On March 7, 1277, Tempier went further and issued a sweeping condemnation of 219 propositions; ten days later, obviously in concert, Archbishop Kilwarby of Canterbury took a similar step. Tempier's 219 propositions are a confused and repetitious list which ranges from ethics to metaphysics. Some of the propositions were only implied rather than explicit in the teaching of the Paris professors. Tempier's chief targets were Siger and the philosophy professors, but his list contains some twenty points taught by Aquinas.

The condemnations of 1277 mark the fundamental turning point in medieval thought. The confidence of Aquinas that Aristotle was in harmony with Christian faith and therefore could provide the substratum for a vast synthesis of philosophy and theology faded rapidly after 1277. New systems arose that downplayed the scientific nature of theology and limited the contribution reason could make to man's knowledge of God, stressing rather the sovereign freedom of the biblical God whom man approaches as a person through the historical covenants revealed in scripture. The thought of the two leading philosopher-theologians of the late middle ages, John Duns Scotus and William of Ockham, reflects the new atmosphere.

Scotus (1266-1308) was a Franciscan who taught at Oxford and Paris. Reflecting a Franciscan emphasis on divine love as manifest in the incarnation and passion of Christ, Scotus reversed the primacy which Aristotle and Aquinas gave to the intellect over the will. For Scotus the will is the whole cause of its own action both in man and in God. At a stroke he cut asunder the Aristotelian identification of intelligibility and necessity. Divine law, including the Ten Commandments, flows from the divine will, not from the divine intellect as for St. Thomas, and binds man because it is commanded, quite apart from any consonance with the created order. Although Scotus gave rational proofs for the existence of God, he severely restricted the power of reason to reach beyond the finite world and denied its power to prove the attributes of God or the immortality of the soul.

Far more radical was the English Franciscan William of Ockham (c. 1290-1349). When his Oxford lectures were attacked, he sought vindication from the pope at Avignon, but there he fell in with the radical Franciscan Michael of Cesena and together they fled to the Emperor Louis the Bavarian, who was at war with the papacy. Ockham spent the last twenty years of his life defending the emperor against the pope in brilliant political tracts. Many of Ockham's finest writings deal with logic and then develop an empiricist theory of knowledge. The knower does not abstract the nature of the object known, rather he knows only the individual object by immediate intuition. Since there are no universal natures but only discrete individual objects, meta-physics is impossible. Since man cannot intuit God nor reach Him by metaphysical argument, rational knowledge of God is impossible. Similarly man cannot conclude to the immortality of the soul nor to its function as the metaphysical form of the body. Clearly Ockham transfers to the realm of faith whole areas that Aquinas put under the power of reason. Precisely because Ockhamist reason knows so little, divine power and will have larger play in his system. Natural events may be due to natural causes, but they may also result from the direct intervention of God. In His absolute power God can do anything not involving a contradiction; for instance, He could declare murder a meritorious act since acts are not good or evil of themselves but only because God has ordered or forbidden them. Given the weakness of reason, revelation becomes the sole source of ethics and theology.

Since Ockham taught that individual things did not share common natures but only were given common names (*nomina*), his disciples were known as nominalists. Their approach was also called the modern way because they opposed the old way of Aquinas and Scotus. By the late fourteenth century the nominalists dominated most universities. Despite the ruthless coherence of Ockhamist thought, nominalism did not stand for religious skepticism or agnosticism; indeed, many later nominalists such as John Gerson and Gabriel Biel are noteworthy for tender piety and pastoral concern. The scholastic tradition which ran from Merton College at Oxford to the University of Padua and Galileo contributed more to the development of scientific method than did renaissance humanism. It was the Paris nominalists Nicholas Oresme and John Buridan who revised Aristotle's theory of motion at critical points. The late middle ages employed many important inventions not known in antiquity, for example, clocks, magnetic compasses, windmills, eye glasses, astrolabes, printing, gun powder and cannons.

Medieval thinkers seldom developed a keen sense of history which would have balanced their speculative bent with a concern for the concrete and circumstantial. Although the nominalists emphasized individuality, their fascination with what might have happened in God's absolute power often distracted them from the real order of salvation revealed in scripture. In philosophy the old way and the new way became rigidly hostile, while in theology the various religious orders tended to follow their own doctors in the spirit of petty rivalry. Late medieval thought lacked the confidence in reason and the joy of discovery that gave the thirteenth century its exuberance. In dealing with scripture medieval theologians generally paid a high price for their concentration on philosophy to the neglect of literature and history, since they often read their Bible as a series of isolated proof texts rather than as organic literary compositions written in specific historical circumstances.

The Towns and the Friars
A Carolingian bishop divided society into the clergy who pray, the nobles who fight, and the peasants who work. This simple division became outmoded when the revival of trade and the population boom fostered the rise of towns in the twelfth century. Even more than the crusades and the universities, the new towns demonstrated the vitality of the age. Some towns grew from the shrunken remains of old Roman cities, others from fortifications and ecclesiastical centers, but many were new foundations in places favorable for trade and defense. In some instances kings and princes founded cities complete with a charter of privileges, but more often the cities had to obtain freedom to regulate their own affairs from feudal overlords. Sometimes they could purchase such charters, but often they had to fight for them. When the overlord was the bishop, the struggle often alienated his people. In Germany and especially in Italy the cities gained almost total independence and self-government, although a circle of patrician families usually controlled politics. In Italy faction-

alism and class struggle allowed petty despots or *Signori* to seize control of most of the cities by the fourteenth century.

The townsfolk did not share the same attitude toward life as the monk and the feudal magnate. They often found irrelevant the old epics and the troubadour tradition of knightly deeds and courtly love; more to their taste was the bawdy humor in Boccaccio's *Decameron* and Chaucer's *Canterbury Tales*, but a craving for God was not absent. Few townsmen approached Dante's learning, much less his poetical skill, but the *Divine Comedy* expressed the longings of many contemporaries. The same passion for a more just society that pulsated through William Langland's *Vision of Piers Plowman* found more humble expression in the charities and bequests for the poor and the suffering which townsfolk made throughout medieval Europe.

Just as the bourgeois needed a new literature, so they required a new pastoral approach. Monastic piety was unsuited to the merchant and his wife in their struggle to raise a family and get ahead in a competitive world. Even less appealing were the abstractions of scholastic philosophy and theology. Among others, St. Bernard, John of Salisbury and Wolfram von Eschenbach had worked out an ideal type of lay Christian in their writings on knighthood. Few nobles lived up to that ideal, which in any case was irrelevant to the townsman, whether merchant prince or lowly weaver.

Making the Gospel real in the towns and cities proved a problem that the medieval church was ill-equipped to handle. Many laymen came to despise the upper clergy for their wealth and the lower clergy for their ignorance. Liturgical worship, so central to the life of the patristic church, carried little of its original force partly because few laymen understood Latin. Gradually the laity ceased to be participants and became spectators; later they busied themselves with private devotions while the priest carried through the rite in splendid isolation. Devotion to the eucharist was strong in the Middle Ages but detoured from reception to gazing on the elevated host. Most laymen received the eucharist only once or twice annually; since they often feared to spill the chalice, the laity gradually came to receive only the host.

Preaching too decayed because so many parish priests were ignorant or lazy. Sermons were seldom effectively tied either to the meaning of the liturgical action or to the scripture readings. Most preaching took place during Advent and especially Lent, when outside friars were imported to give long sermons daily. Towns competed for the services of famous preachers, but the huge audiences and theatrical atmosphere at their sermons only disguised the malaise on the parish level. In the spiritual vacuum there flourished a wide variety of heretical sects. The spiritual crisis of the medieval towns was partly met by the rise of the mendicant friars, especially the Dominicans and Franciscans.

St. Dominic (1170-1221) was a learned Spanish canon who gathered several companions to work for the conversion of the Cathari of southern France by preaching and the example of poverty and holiness. New recruits allowed Dominic to spread his work from Prouille to Toulouse and seek papal approval. His friars were to live on alms and concentrate on preaching. Since preaching required learning, Dominic founded houses in several university towns where Dominican convents had their own carefully devised program of studies, although many friars also became university professors, for instance, St. Thomas Aquinas at Paris.

As early as 1228 there were eleven Dominican provinces from Scandinavia to Palestine. The order was thoroughly international, tightly knit and closely linked to the papacy, which gave it many privileges and called upon its skilled manpower for important tasks, particularly staffing the Inquisition. Local chapters elected local superiors, provincial chapters elected provincials, and annual general chapters elected and helped the master general govern the order. Unlike monasteries which elected their abbots for life, all Dominican superiors except the master general held short term appointments. The Dominicans successfully pioneered government by democracy and administration by committees centuries before they were tried by modern states and corporations. The Dominican reputation for strict poverty, learning, holiness and good government long continued to attract outstanding recruits, mainly from the middle class and university circles.

St. Francis of Assisi (1182-1226) did not have St. Dominic's learning or legislative ability, but he was a peerless charismatic leader who, in Dante's phrase, "rose on the world like a sun." He was a mystic and a poet, who loved the Creator in all creation and joyously modelled his life on Christ with radical simplicity. Even more than St. Bernard, Francis changed the direction of medieval piety to a more direct and tender approach to Christ. It was Francis who first built a Chistmas crib. Prior to him medieval art, especially in Italy, followed the Byzantine tradition of depicting Christ as the Pantocrator, the all powerful judge of the living and the dead. Even on the cross Christ was solemn and triumphant, quite without sign of suffering. Under Franciscan inspiration religious art and devotion came to dwell on God's accessibility through the humanness and suffering of Christ.

In Italy above all the example of St. Francis proved irresistible. Disciples gathered spontaneously, even though St. Francis had no desire to govern or legislate for a great religious order. The first Franciscans were generally poor men, itinerant lay preachers without education. Both St. Francis and Innocent III realized that their religious enthusiasm must be channelled for the good of the church; accordingly Francis wrote an outline rule which Innocent verbally approved in 1209. The early Franciscans expanded this outline during the next fourteen years. Meanwhile St. Francis in declining health withdrew from the governance of the Friars Minor and devoted himself to prayer, but before his death he issued a *Testament* which reaffirmed the strictest personal and corporate poverty.

In fact his ideal of poverty, which forbade even touching money, was nearly impossible as the Franciscans multiplied across the face of Europe, peaking at perhaps 30,000 in 1300. The Franciscans modelled their organization and training on the Dominicans, entered sophisticated apostolates and gained university chairs, while not abandoning the homely street preaching of the first friars. The papacy took over nominal ownership of Franciscan property and provided superiors with dispensations from the strict letter of the rule. By the second half of the thirteenth century the Franciscans were an organized, well-educated order of priests who specialized in foreign missions (China and the Near East), university work, and especially the apostolate to the urban poor. St. Bonaventure presided over this transformation through his writings, his example and his long years as minister general. A faction of Franciscans known as the Spirituals distrusted this evolution, the growing wealth, and the importance of philosophical studies in a band of men dedicated to poverty and simplicity. The appeals of the Spirituals to the letter of the rule and the *Testament* of St. Francis caused constant turmoil in the order and led to papal interventions in its affairs. During the fourteenth century the extreme Spirituals, the Fraticelli, drifted into heresy.

Both St. Dominic and St. Francis founded second orders for cloistered nuns and third orders for laymen, who shared the ideals and devotional life of the friars so far as their work and family duties allowed. Since both Dominicans and Franciscans depended directly on the papacy, many bishops and parish priests resented them as rivals and interlopers.

Heretics and Inquisitors
During its first five centuries the church constantly underwent doctrinal controversy. The New Testament itself is studded with attacks on Gnostic errors. From Constantine to the collapse of the Roman world doctrinal disputes pivoted on the Trinity and the relationship between the human and

the divine in Christ. Although Arianism slowly disappeared after its condemnations at the Councils of Nicaea and Constantinople I, Nestorianism and Monophysitism still survive in the Levant and Ethiopia. In the West St. Augustine opposed the Donatist view that the unworthiness of the minister destroys the validity of the sacraments and the Pelagian heresy that man saves himself by moral effort.

From the Dark Ages to the twelfth century the western church condemned occasional theologians, but no important groups of dissenters arose. This harmony disappeared with the rise of towns, universities and a more sophisticated civilization. In dealing with isolated intellectuals the medieval church was relatively lenient—no university professor was executed for his views from 1150 to 1300—but faced with dissident groups the church became unrelenting and pitiless.

Catharism offered the most serious doctrinal challenge to the medieval church. Probably Catharism should not even be classified as a Christian heresy since it shared less with Christianity than do Islam and Judaism. The Cathari, or pure ones (also called Albigenses from their center at Albi near Toulouse), revived Manicheanism which postulated two fundamental principles in cosmic struggle. The god of light, who creates everything spiritual and good, battles the god of darkness, who creates matter and evil. In some versions, the evil god is a fallen son or angel of the good god, but increasingly the thesis of two uncreated primordial principles gained ground. The Cathari accepted much of the Bible but gave it an allegorical interpretation so that Christ was an angel with a phantom body who redeems man by his teaching. His passion and death have no significance for salvation. Men are spirits imprisoned in evil matter for the sins of a previous life. Obviously there can be no resurrection of the body for Christ or the saved. The use of meat, milk, and eggs is evil, as also the use of sex for procreation.

Catharism, which filtered into the West about 1140 from the Bogomils of Bulgaria who seem directly linked to the ancient Manicheans, first spread in the commercial cities of northern Italy but gained its greatest strength in southern France, with pockets through southern Germany. Everywhere it capitalized on the wealth and corruption of the Catholic clergy. The Cathari developed a liturgy which imitated the eucharist, but their basic sacrament was the *consolamentum*, a sort of baptism, whose reception separated the Perfect from the mass of mere believers. The Perfect lived in great austerity, keeping rigorous dietary and sexual prohibitions; not a few sought release from the prison of the flesh by voluntary starvation. On the other hand the believers led ordinary lives (or extraordinarily dissolute lives if Catholic charges are accepted), meanwhile hoping to receive the *consolamentum* shortly before death.

During the twelfth century the popes tried to stamp out Catharism by formal condemnations and by dispatching preachers to the affected areas, but these efforts had little success. After the murder in 1208 of a papal legate to southern France, Innocent III determined on drastic measures and laid the groundwork for the papal Inquisition to circumvent the leniency of local civil and ecclesiastical judges. He also encouraged a crusade by land-hungry nobles from northern France, who crushed both the Cathari and sympathetic southern nobles such as the Count of Toulouse. The northerners then took over their land and helped the Inquisition stamp out Catharism.

Pantheism, which identifies God with the universe, fascinated many medieval thinkers. The writings of Scotus Erigena, Meister Eckhart and Nicholas of Cusa contain statements with a pantheistic ring, but it is very doubtful that they were pantheists. Amaury of Bène, a leading professor at Paris in the opening years of the thirteenth century, taught a mystical pantheism which attracted a core of disciples. Eleven of them, all clerics, were burned at Paris in 1210 after they refused to recant. Despite repeated condemnations the Amaurians (or Amalricians) continued to spread in the

French trading towns. One of their leaders told his captors that "he could neither be consumed by fire nor tormented by torture, for in so far as he was, he was God." Other Amaurians drew the conclusions that since they were identical with God, they could not sin and were not bound by moral laws. During the fourteenth century similar views prevailed among the amorphous Brethren of the Free Spirit and penetrated various groups of Beguines, women who modelled their life on nuns but without taking vows or entering a formal religious order.

Very different was Joachim (c. 1132-1202), the abbot of Flora in the toe of Italy, who died revered for sanctity after submitting his writings to the judgment of the church. In fact several of his writings proclaimed a salvation history radically different from the Old and New Testaments. Starting from the doctrine of the Trinity, Joachim theorized that just as there had been the era of the Father in the Old Testament and the New Covenant in the saving blood of Christ, so a third and final dispensation of the Holy Spirit was about to dawn on the world. What might have passed as the apocalyptic ravings of a harmless old man were picked up by the extreme Spiritual Franciscans, who saw Joachim himself as the precursor of the new era, with St. Francis and the new religious orders bringing on the era of the Holy Spirit. The Spirituals saw themselves as the new spiritual church which supplants the hierarchy of the second covenant just as it supplanted the Jewish high priests; accordingly they felt they could ignore papal condemnations of their insistance on absolute poverty for the church. Among the lower classes of Italy a simplified Joachism gave ideological support to anticlericalism, whereas in Germany Joachite ideas merged with popular expectations of a second coming of Emperor Frederick II to chastise wicked clergymen.

Other medieval heresies ignored high-blown speculation and combined denunciations of the clergy with a demand for a return to the Bible. This approach is well exemplified by the

Waldensians. Their founder was Peter Waldo (also Valdo and Valdes), a rich merchant of Lyons who, heart-struck by Christ's call to the rich young man, distributed his property to the poor and became a wandering preacher in 1173. Like his younger contemporary, Francis of Assisi, he attracted disciples, the Poor Men of Lyons, who denounced the wealth and corruption of the clergy and circulated Bible translations. At first the papacy gave them cautious support, but they seemed unruly, ignorant and dangerous to many bishops. Even after Lucius III condemned them, their preaching spread in France, Piedmont on both sides of the Alps, and parts of Germany, Spain and Bohemia. Some of their preachers returned to Catholicism in the early thirteenth century but most of them moved to a fundamental rejection of the Catholic church as corrupt. Indeed with the Fraticelli they came to see the pope as anti-Christ. They rejected the cult of the saints, purgatory and many Catholic practices as superstitious. Persecution disrupted their corporate existence in most areas, but they continued to survive in the mountainous areas of France and Italy. In the sixteenth century they established close links with Calvinism, which enabled them to survive renewed persecution. Today the Waldensians number some 20,000, chiefly in northern Italy.

Both the life and teaching of Waldo remain shadowy compared to those of John Wyclif (1330-1384), the Oxford reformer. More than forty volumes of his writings remain, mostly Latin works of scholastic philosophy and theology in a prolix and obscure style that limited their impact. He attacked the nominalist and Pelagian views of his Oxford colleagues, but he only aroused intense opposition when he bitterly denounced clerical failings. He joined his attack with a radical theory of dominion which taught that only men possessing grace have the right to exercise authority and hold property. In the first instance his theory was aimed at sinful churchmen, but its political and social implications were enormous. Wyclif had little to do with the Peasants Revolt

of 1381, but his ideas were blamed. His doctrine of the eucharist foreshadows the teaching of Luther and Calvin. Both
the pope and the archbishop of Canterbury replied with condemnations which drove Wyclif and many followers from
Oxford, but the protection of John of Gaunt, Duke of Lan-
caster, enabled him to retire unmolested to his parish at Lut-
terworth. In 1415 the Council of Constance condemned 267
statements culled from his writings.

It is doubtful how much Wyclif really influenced the Lollards, the English dissenters who claimed him as patron. Certainly he taught that religion should be drawn from the Bible
alone and encouraged an English translation, but whether he
actually translated any of the Lollard Bible remains dubious.
His writings anticipate the teachings of the later Protestant
reformers but exercised little influence on them. When active
persecutions started in 1401, most academic Lollards re-
canted and the movement was confined to lower class dissenters. Underground pockets survived until the Reformation
when they merged with early English and Scotch Protestantism.

Ironically Wyclif probably had his greatest influence in
Bohemia, which was linked to England by royal marriage.
Czech students returning from Oxford brought back his writings, which found fertile soil in university circles at Prague,
because of the usual anticlericalism and because the Czechs
resented German influence at the University. Among the
Czech Wyclifites John Hus (c. 1369-1415) was certainly the
most eloquent and popular but by no means the most radical.
Hus avoided Wyclif's eucharistic teaching but accepted his
reform ideas and his understanding of the church as the community of the predestined. Hus also rejected papal primacy
of jurisdiction, which was not yet a defined doctrine of Catholicism. When his preaching led to excommunication
and an interdict which stopped the administration of the sacraments in Prague, Hus left the city and spent two years
evangelizing the countryside with great effect. He then vol-

untarily answered a summons to the Council of Constance, naively trusting in the Emperor's promise of safe conduct and his own ability to convince the Council. At Constance he defended the condemned doctrines of Wyclif, whereupon the Council condemned him too and handed him over to the Emperor Sigismund for execution.

The burning of Hus drove the Czechs into rebellion. Although the pope preached a crusade against the heretic nation and Sigismund, king of Bohemia after 1419, recruited an army of Germans, the Czech lower classes rallied to the Hussite banner and under their remarkable generals John Zizka and Prokop the Great smashed the invading Germans. In the moment of victory the Hussites split into factions: the Utraquists insisted on communion under both bread and wine (*sub utraque*) but sought a compromise with the Catholics, whereas the Taborites (from their headquarters at Tabor), who represented the militant lower classes, refused all compromise, upheld Wyclif's more radical doctrines, and demanded that all doctrine and practice must be measured against a literal interpretation of the New Testament. Thereupon the Catholics and Utraquists combined to defeat the Taborites. For a period the popes granted the Czechs communion under both bread and wine, but relations between Bohemia and Rome were strained and irregular right down to the German reformation, when most of the country went over to Lutheranism.

In the early Middle Ages there was little heresy and only scattered local inquisitions under the bishops. The rise of the Cathari and Waldensians induced a defensive psychology among Catholics which led to a spate of papal legislation against heresy. The most fundamental was Gregory IX's constitution of 1231 which organized the papal Inquisition and demanded that the state execute obstinate heretics. The medieval Inquisition was most active in France, southern Germany and northern Italy. The inquisitors, usually trained theologians from the Dominicans and Franciscans, had wide powers to summon suspects for investigation. In some areas the Inquisition had popular support, but in many places it was resented and could not count on cooperation from government officials. In a few cases the heretics struck back and assassinated inquisitors such as Conrad of Marburg and Peter of Verona.

Even in an age when civil courts gave the accused few rights and used torture, the Inquisition employed exceptional procedures. The accused could not face his accusers and had no effective right to a lawyer; he was obliged to answer under oath, even though his testimony might incriminate himself, his friends and his relatives; and he could be tortured. There is no evidence to believe lurid popular accounts of widespread sadism, nor did the right of Inquisition to share in the confiscated property give rise to general abuse. Ultimately the Inquisition must be condemned on more fundamental grounds: that it imposed·punishment for religious deviation (mainly doctrinal, but also moral), even though the churchmen and theologians responsible insisted that faith was a free gift of God which no man could gain by his own desire, much less by coercion. Certainly they found no justification in the New Testament. How, then, did Christians come to approve such a perversion of Christianity?

Since Constantine and the conversion of the Roman world there grew up the concept of Christendom as a united bloc of peoples sharing a common religion and culture. To be sure, there were non-Christians within Christendom; the Jews, for instance, enjoyed official toleration although they were often treated unjustly. But for most people birth into Christendom was swiftly followed by baptism and incorporation into the church. Canonists and theologians made an all-too-facile link between baptism and faith, so that any baptized person who later rejected an article of faith was seen as deliberately sinning against the light. Should the heretic try to win others to his convictions, he was insulting God, increasing his own guilt, and jeopardizing his neighbor's eternal salvation. By comparison the well poisoner only endangered temporal life. Should not heresy receive the same punishment as murder? Medieval jurists did not see heresy as bringing only spiritual harm: since the fabric of medieval society rested on religion, the heretic posed a threat to the state and society no less than to the church. Consequently most medieval governments had civil laws which imposed the death penalty for heresy. For medieval Christians the very type of heresy was Catharism, which indeed threatened medieval civilization. Medieval anti-heresy laws, moreover, functioned as self-fulfilling prophecy, for once the law equated the heretic with the rebel, then revolution was the heretic's only road to escape persecution. Right down to the seventeenth century social protest movements rather consistently took on a theological rationale, thus confirming the establishment's identification of heresy with rebellion.

3

Decay in the Church

The Black Death

In 1344 the Tartars beseiged the remote Genoese trading post of Caffa in the Crimea. After two years of fighting, plague broke out in both the crowded town and the squalid Tartar camp. The Tartars broke off the seige and carried the plague eastward toward India. By 1352 the Black Death was killing millions in China. Many of the Caffa defenders sailed home to Genoa. Two days after their ship docked plague symptoms appeared in the port. The Black Death, the greatest catastrophe in human history, had begun its irresistible march across Europe.

The Black Death consisted of three plagues, bubonic, pneumonic and septicemic, which have distinct symptoms but work in concert. Most basic is bubonic which is spread to man by fleas which normally inhabit black rats. Black rats, seemingly unknown to antiquity and now largely replaced by the more ferocious brown rat, have an unfortunate affinity for human settlements, so that fleas from infected rats easily spread to men. The chief symptom of bubonic plague is the buboes or egg-sized swellings near the lymph glands, usually under the armpits or in the groin. The victim is usually dead within three days. Pneumonic plague is even more lethal since there is no immunity. Unlike bubonic plague, its bacilli spread from man to man through coughing or infected clothing. In the Black Death the pneumonic bacilli started slower than the bubonic, but later became the main killer since they spread independently of rats and fleas. Finally septicemic plague accompanied the epidemic at its height, directly attacking the blood stream and killing within hours. Medieval medicine had no remedies for the Black Death and did not even understand the fatal rats-fleas-men linkage.

In general the Black Death was worst in populous areas so that northern Italy and France suffered more than Spain and Germany. Cities suffered more than towns, towns more than the countryside. In the trading city of Bremen mortality reached seventy percent; Europe as a whole by conservative estimate lost a quarter of its population. Had the Black Death been a single massive blow, recovery could have taken place in a few decades, but the original Black Death was followed by new outbreaks in 1360, 1369 and 1375. In England these new epidemics carried off respectively twenty-three, thirteen and thirteen percent of the population. The plague was particularly severe on the elderly, but more important was the high mortality among children, which jeopardized the future. Generally the poor were hardest hit because the rich had better food and better hygiene, were less exposed to contact with rats and could flee the outbreak, as did the wealthy men and women who relate the tales in Boccaccio's *Decameron*, whose opening pages give an eye-witness account of the Black Death in Florence.

High population and bad harvests doubtless increased mortality in 1348, but the Black Death cannot be explained simply as a Malthusian crisis brought on because European population was straining against the limits of food production. The epidemic affected Africa and Asia as well as Europe. In some European areas the population seems to have leveled off or declined two decades before the Black Death; elsewhere there were still resources for an expanding population in 1348. The thesis of a population crisis does not easily explain the renewed attacks in 1360, 1369 and 1375 nor the low and unresponsive birth rate thereafter which delayed full recovery of the population for two centuries.

Even for the people who escaped the disease, its effects were shattering. Some underwent religious conversions to expiate their sins, avert God's wrath, or prepare for eternity. More often the approach of the plague had the opposite effect, as men squandered their money in drinking and debauchery. Extraordinary strain snapped the bonds of duty, decency and social restraint in men of weak character. Others sacrificed themselves to the service of the sick, realizing that they were sure to catch the contagion. Most men were bewildered by the catastrophe which no medicine and no precaution seemed able to alleviate. Clearly, it seemed, God was emptying the vials of His wrath on sinful mankind. The mass, the sacraments, special prayers and processions seemed powerless to appease God's anger. Some men lost confidence in traditional piety; but others drew the psychological comfort that they were doing something to slow the spreading epidemic. In desperation men looked to scapegoats: strangers and lepers were accused of poisoning wells and were executed. In Christian Spain the victims were Moslems, but elsewhere the Jews were the main scapegoats. Traditional anti-Semitism, greed, the resentment of debtors and mass hysteria overrode the efforts of rulers and even a papal excommunication which tried to protect the Jews. The massacre at Strasbourg, which had a very large Jewish community, may have claimed eight thousand. When it became clear that killing Jews did nothing to stop the plague, the pogroms abated, but here and there they were sparked anew by the arrival of anti-Semitic flagellants.

The flagellant bands were both the most curious and characteristic psychological reaction to the Black Death. Self-flagellation can be found among people of nearly every age and enjoyed some vogue as monastic self-mortification, but mass flagellation began in Eastern Europe in 1348 and spread through Germany; elsewhere it was less popular. Unconcious

eroticism may have played a role, but the chief motive of the
Brotherhood of the Flagellants was to take upon themselves
the sins of the community and appease divine wrath. Except
for occasional hymns, the flagellant bands marched silently,
two by two, three hundred to a thousand strong, snaking
from town to town and spreading the plague they sought to
avert. In each town they formed a circle in the marketplace,
stripped off their heavy cowls and red-crossed gowns down
to a linen shirt; first they lay in prayer, then rose thrice to
scourge themselves bloody with leather whips studded with
nails. The whole performance was repeated twice by day and
once by night. Each flagellant vowed thirty-three days'
service and promised not to bathe or change his blood-clot-
ted clothing. The flagellant mortality rate must have been
staggering. As each flagellant had to have money in advance
for his expenses, the very poor were excluded, as were most
clergy. Gradually the movement turned against the rich and
the clergy. The flagellants despised the usual church minis-
trations and their own masters gave absolution. Eventually
the pope denounced them for disrupting church discipline,
and the rulers turned against them. As the Black Death
waned, so did the Flagellant Brotherhood, only to flare up
here and there with the return of plague.

The Black Death contributed greatly to the pessimism, the
fixation on death and the keen sense of life as fleeting which
permeated the late medieval world. Concern with purgatory,
indulgences and masses for the dead increased. The impact
was evident in religious art; for instance, in Tuscany the
majestic naturalism of Giotto, the delicate harmony of
Duccio and the courtly grace of Simone Martini gave way to
Traini's *Triumph of Death* in the Pisa graveyard, which contrasts self-concious frivolity with putrifying corpses and
issues a summons to repentance. Art returned to a simplified
symbolism and a more rigid, hieractic arrangement of
figures. Drawings and woodcuts of the dance of death

continued popular right down to the series done by young Holbein. The art of Hieronymus Bosch with its private symbolism and grotesque imagination seems utterly idiosyncratic, but his pessimistic moralism typifies the late Middle Ages in northern Europe. Even his contemporary, Hans Memling, the master of gentle elegy, has left us a terrifying *Last Judgement.*

Unlike war which destroys both men and property, the plague left property intact. The survivors inherited from the dead; they may have been richer, but the plague unsettled economic and social relationships. Initially there was a labor shortage and since people had greater wealth, a period of prosperity and higher wages ensued. Marginal land went out of cultivation; indeed, whole villages were abandoned. But bust soon followed boom since fewer consumers meant smaller markets. When the upper classes tried to impose low wages and old obligations, popular insurrections followed. The French Jacquerie of 1358, the English Peasants' revolt of 1381, the Ciompi rising in Florence in 1378 are only the most famous. Generally the Black Death and its aftermath brought the peasants of western Europe greater freedom and higher wages, but in eastern Europe the nobles proved stronger and tightened peasant servitude. In the cities unsettled conditions and the need to cut costs by lowering wages helped depress the working class to subsistence.

The church suffered from the Black Death more than other institutions. The best pastors stayed with their flocks and died serving the stricken, while the worst priests fled and survived. The crisis also seems to have weakened monastic discipline. There are indications that the death rate among the clergy was even higher than among the laity. The thousands of benefices and church jobs left open were filled either by mass ordination of young, poorly trained clerics or by pluralism—one man holding several benefices. Both left an evil legacy.

Political Changes

The Hundred Years' War and its consequences dominate the political history of northern Europe in the fourteenth and fifteenth centuries. The war directly involved France, England, Scotland and the Low Countries, but touched Germany and Spain as well. It began in 1338 and petered out in 1453 without a formal peace treaty, but fighting was by no means continuous. The basic cause of the war was England's feudal possessions in France, particularly Guienne, together with the English dynastic claims to the French crown itself. The dependance of Flanders on English wool and Scotland's reliance on France against English encroachment complicated the issues. Most of the war involved mercenary bands pillaging the French countryside with little concern for larger questions. In the great set-piece battles of Crécy, Poitiers and Agincourt English tactics and the longbow cut down great masses of French knights in their foolish gallantry, but ultimately England could not win. France was larger and far more populous; she was fighting on her own soil for national survival, while the English kings were fighting for glory and the French crown. England's hopes depended on the support of her French vassals and her Burgundian allies, but her hold on them weakened as the decades of war sharpened French national spirit. Brilliant victories stirred the pride of Englishmen, but people and Parliament grew restive under the endless drain of blood and gold to the battlefields of France.

The power of French national spirit emerges from the strangest episode of the war, the career of St. Joan of Arc (1412-1431). The story of the peasant girl whom her voices summoned to rescue France from the triumphant English is too well known to recount here. At first Joan seems a completely medieval figure; in fact she foreshadows the modern world, not because she anticipates women's liberation by donning armour and succeeding at the masculine enterprise of war, but because she identified the cause of her fatherland with the will of God: emblazoning *Gott mit uns* on the equipment of the *national* army is more modern than medieval. Precisely because Joan claimed to be God's instrument, her English captors had to discredit her utterly by charges of heresy and sorcery, a long show trial and a public burning.

Loyalty to the nation grew at the expense of older loyalties—to the feudal lord, the local district and to Christendom as a whole. The rising nationalism compromised the church, whose structure was at once more local and international than national. Increasingly the early national state tried to control the church by taking over major appointments and restricting papal intervention. Englishmen exaggerated the influence of the French crown on the French popes at Avignon and passed the Statues of Praemunire which prevented appeals to the papal curia. In 1438 Charles VII of France unilaterally issued the Pragmatic Sanction of Bourges which deprived the pope of the right to tax French clergymen, declared the administrative autonomy of the French church and largely put the appointment of French bishops under the crown.

The fifteenth century was not a glorious age in German history. The age lacks a dominant movement, institution or personality around which to weave an account. The Swiss Confederation and the Netherlands ever more clearly freed themselves from imperial overlordship. The free imperial cities in the south and the Rhineland, prosperous from trade, mining and banking, developed a patriciate which imitated the culture of renaissance Italy with considerable success. Emperor Maximilian I (1493-1519), who presided over the last generation of medieval Germany, dreamt of mighty projects including election as pope but lacked resources and persistence. Many of his wars ended in defeat and his reforms accomplished little, but he did arrange a series of marriages that secured for his grandson, Charles V, an empire unmatched since Charlemagne.

In January 1469 Isabella, heiress of Castile, made the most momentous decision in Spanish history. She defied her royal

brother who wanted her to marry the old widower king of
Portugal, Alfonso V; instead she arranged a wedding with
Ferdinand, the young and energetic heir of Aragon. Her
choice soon involved her in a war against Portugal, but
Ferdinand's intelligence and Aragonese help brought Isabella
victory. Had Isabella chosen Alfonso or lost the war, Castile
would have been united to Portugal, and her interests would
have turned toward the Atlantic where the Portuguese sea-
men of Henry the Navigator had already made important
discoveries. Instead Castile was linked to Aragon and
through Aragon to Italy and the Mediterranean. Aragon
already occupied Sardinia and Sicily, and Ferdinand re-established control over the Kingdom of Naples against French
claims, thereby founding two centuries of Spanish hegemony
over Italy.

The most important year in Spanish history was 1492. Not
only did Columbus begin Spain's career of exploration and
colonization in Latin America, but Ferdinand and Isabella
completed the conquest of Granada, the last Moslem foot-
hold. Less than three months later they took a further, tragic
step to unify Spain by ordering the expulsion of the Jews.

During most of the Middle Ages Moslems, Jews and
Christians dwelt together in the Iberian peninsula with considerable harmony, each enriching the culture of the others,
but anti-Jewish riots swept Spain in 1391, so that nearly half
the Spanish Jews accepted baptism in fear of their lives.
Many converted Jews or *conversos* prospered in business and
government to such a degree that both the old aristocracy
and the lower classes grew to resent them. Some *conversos*
were insincere Christians who easily slipped back to the religion of their fathers, but others became Christian zealots. In
1478 Ferdinand and Isabella obtained from Rome a special
Spanish Inquisition under royal control to deal with back-
sliding *conversos*. The expulsion of the Jews from Spain was
later decreed to lessen the temptation of weak *conversos*.
Indeed, zealot *conversos* urged both measures. The

monarchs themselves acted from a curious mixture of pious bigotry and reasons of state; they felt that a country diverse in language, law, customs and history needed religious unity. Indeed, Castile and Aragon had only two common institutions, the monarchy and the Inquisition. In 1492 nearly 150,000 Jews left Spain, mainly for Africa, Italy and the Levant, taking with them their wealth and their skills. Since many Jews chose baptism over exile, the expulsion compounded the problem it was supposed to solve. Two years later Ferdinand and Isabella, dissatisfied by the slow pace of conversion among their Moorish subjects, offered Moslems a grim alternative: conversion or exile. For the poor there was no practical alternative to baptism, which brought them under the jurisdiction of the Inquisition. Henceforward every Spaniard was a Christian by law, but a century of sporadic Morisco revolts and mutual atrocities showed that religion cannot be legislated.

The leading churchman in the Spain of Ferdinand and Isabella was the austere Franciscan, Francisco Ximenes de Cisneros (1437-1517), under whose direction the Spanish church made serious efforts at reform. First as Isabella's confessor, then as Cardinal primate of Toledo, and finally as regent, Ximenes made excellent use of the unprecedented power over the church which Rome granted the monarchs by the Concordat of 1482. He must also share the blame for their Morisco policy. Nowhere was he more drastic and successful than in reforming his fellow Franciscans. Rather than practice strict celibacy, four hundred Andalusian friars converted to Islam and sailed for Africa with their women. No humanist himself, Ximenes founded the University of Alcalá with a humanist curriculum and sponsored the Alcalá Bible, which in 1516 printed parallel texts in Hebrew, Greek and Latin for instant comparison.

During the thirteenth century northern Italy was a mosaic of merchant republics, but growing factionalism allowed petty despots to take over most cities. Only with difficulty did the Tuscan cities of Florence, Siena and Lucca remain republics. Venice, thanks to her peculiar geography and compact aristocracy, stood serene and aloof from the factionalism that wracked other republics. Increasingly after 1350 the larger states absorbed their smaller neighbors. Gian Galeazzo Visconti of Milan came close to consolidating all northern Italy before his unexpected death in 1402, whereupon Venice took advantage of Milanese weakness to occupy territory around the head of the Adriatic. In 1454 the Peace of Lodi ended fifty years of struggle between Milan and Venice and established a balance of power that insured an era of peace, prosperity and cultural flowering. In 1494 Charles VIII of France invaded Italy to claim Naples, which he easily conquered, but his success drove the Italians into coalition with Ferdinand of Aragon. Charles barely extricated his army from Italy, but later Louis XII and Francis I renewed French claims to Naples and Milan. Their invasions only squandered French resources, devastated the country, and increased Spanish control of Italy.

The Failure of Conciliarism

The decline of the medieval papacy is usually traced from the pontificate of Boniface VIII (1294-1303), a headstrong canon lawyer who opposed the efforts of Philip IV of France and Edward I of England to tax their clergy. Boniface drew up a series of decrees which asserted papal claims in magniloquent terms, while Philip replied by a propaganda campaign which accused Boniface of heresy, adultery, the murder of Celestine V, illegal election as pope and even of keeping a private demon as a house pet. Philip then sent a band of ruffians to arrest Boniface and haul him to France for trial. At Anagni they seized and manhandled the aged pontiff, who died several weeks later.

The new pope Benedict XI had no stomach for struggle and hastened to placate Philip. Within eight months Benedict died and the conclave of cardinals deadlocked for eleven months before electing Clement V, the archbishop of Bordeaux. Clement, an indecisive hypochondriac, settled temporarily at Avignon, a papal enclave, to be on hand for the ecumenical council at nearby Vienne in 1312. Philip tried to use the council to convict Boniface VIII and suppress the Knights of Templar for their wealth. To save Boniface from condemnation, Clement V accepted the confessions wrung from the Templars by Philip's torturers and allowed their suppression. Clement appointed French cardinals, who elected a French pope, who in turn appointed more French cardinals. Seven popes lived at Avignon from 1309 to 1378, partly because it was a pleasant spot and more centrally located than Rome, but mainly because central Italy was turbulent and Rome was dominated by the great noble families who traditionally opposed the popes. All the Avignon popes realized that Rome, with its traditions and the bones of the saints, was their proper home, that by tarrying at Avignon they were setting an example of absenteeism and losing prestige. Three times the popes called off a return to Italy at the last minute. Despite Clement V's abject surrender to Philip IV, most of the Avignon popes were not lackeys of the French crown. Although not outstanding for piety, they possessed exceptional gifts for financial administration; since the papal states no longer contributed much income, the Avignon popes developed elaborate taxes on the various appointments, dispensations and documents that they provided for clergymen throughout Christendom. Ultimately the cost was passed on to the laity. The financial machinery developed at Avignon returned with the popes to Rome and continued to sharpen hostility to the papacy for centuries.

Gregory XI died shortly after his return to Rome in 1378. When the cardinals gathered to elect a new pope, the Roman mob screamed for a Roman or at least an Italian. How much the cardinals were intimidated is still debated, but at any rate they elected an Italian archbishop. Urban VI immediately showed himself an autocratic reformer. Shocked, most of the cardinals fled to Anagni and elected a second pope, Clement VII, on the grounds that the first election lacked freedom. Clement took up residence at Avignon. Urban excommunicated Clement and his supporters, and Clement returned the courtesy. Both popes appointed cardinals, who in turn elected new popes at both Rome and Avignon. Who was the rightful pope? Historians favor the Roman line, but since the evidence for both sides was dubious, contemporaries gave their allegiance on political grounds. France and her allies favored Avignon; conversely England, Portugal and much of Germany and Italy supported Rome. In a few places rival appointees carried the schism down to the diocesan and parish level.

Everybody recognized that there was only one legitimate pope, but solving the debacle was not so easy. Mutual abdication and the election of a neutral seemed the best way, but egoism, politics and legal technicalities snagged several attempts at this solution. Increasingly churchmen, lawyers and royal counsellors looked to an ecumenical council to end the scandal of two popes. The Paris theologians took the lead in reviving conciliarism, the theory that ecumenical councils were superior to the popes since they represented all Christians and that accordingly they should play a regular role in governing and reforming the church. Conciliarism raised a hornets' nest of theological problems, but the need for action outstripped their resolution. Five hundred prelates held a council at Pisa which deposed both popes as heretics and commissioned the election of Alexander V. The popes at Rome and Avignon excommunicated Alexander, who shortly died and was succeeded by a disreputable adventurer. Obviously the council at Pisa had intensified the problem.

At this juncture the conciliarist theologians called on Emperor Sigismund to play the role of Constantine and supervise a new council. Sigismund, happy to heal the schism and raise imperial prestige, convened the Council of Constance (1414-1418) which secured the resignations of the

Pisan and Roman popes and deposed the Avignon claimant. The election of Martin V, who took up residence in Rome, ended the schism. The Council of Constance also tried to deal with the problem of Wyclif and Hus, then turned to the immense task of reforming the church in head and members. Nearly everybody acknowledged the need for reform in the abstract, but most concrete reforms cut against powerful vested interests. The bishops wanted a restoration of their powers which had been undermined by privileges and dispensations that the popes had given religious orders and individuals. The pope and the orders opposed that reform. Theoretically cathedral chapters should elect bishops; in fact the kings chose most bishops and used this power to reward their civil servants at the expense of the church. Without royal cooperation reform was empty talk, but no king was willing to surrender control over his episcopacy. Throughout Europe nobles and gentry had acquired the right to nominate abbots, priors and pastors; family connections determined nominations more often than ability or sanctity. Indeed, the whole benefice system of paying the clergy, into which the church had slipped so naturally in the feudal period, was outmoded, inefficient, and rife with abuse by 1400, yet the system was woven into such a web of vested interests that no fundamental reform was possible until the new industrial world after the French revolution.

The conciliarists at Constance argued that the best instrument for reform was frequent ecumenical councils; they embodied their conviction in two decrees: *Sacrosancta* which asserted the power of the councils over the whole church including the pope, and *Frequens* which set up frequent meetings of future councils to supervise reform. Obviously the conciliarist program reduced the pope to an interim executive officer of omnipotent and recurrent councils. The popes refused to accept this part of the conciliar reform program. For the next hundred years the popes struggled to head off conciliarism; conversely appeals to the next council became

a familiar weapon for the enemies of the papacy. As conciliarists and papalists maneuvered, practical reform stagnated.

In 1431 an ecumenical council met at Basel after an abor-
tive attempt to convene at Pavia. It entered promising negotiations with the Hussites but soon became so divided by
national jealousies and divergent views on the papacy and reform that its prestige suffered. Meanwhile the Byzantine
emperor, hardpressed by the Ottoman Turks and needing
western help, bypassed the Council of Basel and applied
directly to Pope Eugenius IV to convene a council that could
negotiate the reunion of the eastern and western churches.
Eugenius ordered the council at Basel to reconvene at Ferrara
to meet the Byzantine delegates. The moderates at Basel
complied, but the extremists refused and declared Eugenius a
heretic and elected Felix V as antipope. This foolhardy action destroyed the council's last authority. Conciliarism was
dead as a practical movement.

In March 1438 eight hundred Greeks, including Emperor
John VIII, the patriarch of Constantinople, and twenty metropolitans, arrived at Ferrara to begin reunion discussions.
Eleven months later the council moved to Florence when the
queen city of the renaissance promised to subsidize its expenses. The emperor wanted concrete pledges of military
help, but most western princes ignored the council. The
Greeks started the theological discussions by attacking the
teaching of the Latin church that the Holy Spirit proceeds not
only from the Father but also from the Son. After months of
heated debate the Greeks came to accept the Latin formula-
tion as equivalent to the traditional Greek teaching that the
Spirit proceeds from the Father through the Son. Agreement
came more easily on purgatory and papal primacy, which
were the other doctrinal differences between east and west. In
July 1439 the pope and the emperor together with their
bishops signed the decree of reunion *Laetentur Caeli*. Only
Bishop Mark of Ephesus, the leading Greek theologian, refused his signature. Rome soon reached supplementary
agreements with the Armenians, Copts and Maronites.

The reunion proved short-lived. The Byzantine people continued to regard the Latins as heretics, especially after the writings of Mark of Ephesus stiffened their opposition and swung around many bishops. The emperor was in a weak position to impose the union since he had no binding promise of military aid. The defeat and death of King Ladislas of Poland and Hungary with his crusaders at Varna in 1444 destroyed the last real hope for church union and for the Byzantine Empire. Nine years later massive Turkish cannons breached the walls that had withstood so many sieges. Mohammed II made Constantinople his capital and employed its patriarch to help govern the Christians of the Levant and the Balkans.

The popes during the eighty years that separated the Council of Florence from the Protestant reformation were mostly men of culture and intelligence, but their moral level descended to that of the petty despots against whom they contended for control of central Italy. Even the scarlet sins of Alexander VI, who sired seven illegitimate children as a young man, should not distract attention from the fundamental failing of the renaissance popes—that they lost their sense of service to God and His people. Again and again they neglected the universal church to advance family interests or consolidate their authority in the papal states. Alexander VI's attempt to carve out a principality for his vicious son Cesare Borgia has attracted notice ever since Machiavelli's *The Prince*, but other renaissance popes before and after Alexander made similar efforts. Julius II (1503-1513), who personally led his armies in full armour and patronized Raphael and Michelangelo, tried to free Italy from foreign domination and was perhaps right in thinking that the popes could deal with the princes as equals only when they had a secure political base; but his military exploits and devious diplomacy (first as France's ally against Venice, then supporting Venice against France) disgusted not only the pacific Erasmus but even the cynical historian Guicciardini. Julius was a virtuoso at power politics, but the papacy was bound to lose once it played.the game of princes. When the popes tried to speak in their other role as spiritual leaders of Christendom, their deeds belied their words. Nothing corrodes religion like hypocrisy, and renaissance Rome reeked with hypocrisy.

The renaissance popes were invariably former cardinals. Usually the cardinals elected Italians, but two Spaniards and a Dutchman attained the tiara between 1455 and 1523. Theoretically the cardinals were the senior officials of the church's central administration, but increasingly they were members of leading Italian families, key transalpine bishops, and relatives of past and present popes. Sixtus IV raised six of his worthless nephews to the cardinalate. While there were conscientious administrators among the cardinals, too many devoted their energies to scrambling for bishoprics whose income would allow them to maintain palaces and patronize the arts.

At the beginning of the sixteenth century Rome replaced Florence as the center of Renaissance art. For nearly two centuries Florence dominated the artistic and intellectual life of Italy, until the French invasion of 1494 led to the expulsion of the Medici and the rise of Savonarola. That fiery Dominican preacher not only touched the hearts of ordinary citizens but profoundly influenced the philosopher Giovanni Pico della Mirandola and young Michelangelo. Even Sandro Botticelli, famed for his idyllic *Birth of Venus*, turned to painting anguished pietàs. But the re-established Florentine republic, neither during Savonarola's regime of penitence nor after his execution, could offer patronage on the scale that Julius II and Leo X provided. By 1514 Raphael, Michelangelo and Bramante had created at Rome the characteristic masterpieces of the high renaissance; even Leonardo da Vinci came to Rome, but more to brood than to paint. Raphael's *School of Athens* and *Disputà* capture for all time the Renaissance coordination of reason and revelation, of classicism and Christianity, just as Michelangelo's Sistine ceiling raises a matchless paean to the majesty of God and the dignity of man.

Ironically the *terribilità* of Julius II and the oily refinement of Leo X, which helped to make them unsurpassed art patrons, also crippled them as spiritual leaders on the eve of the reformation.

The Medieval Bible

The Bible is the constant fount of Christian doctrine and inspiration. How important was it during the Middle Ages? No easy answer is possible. Although the Bible was the most studied book in the Middle Ages, most medieval men never saw a page and most medieval priests had only a superficial knowledge. Obviously a low literacy rate hampered Bible reading, as did the extreme expense of books before the invention of rag paper and printing. It took three hundred sheep skins to make parchment for one Bible and over a year's copying for a skilled scribe. The price of a manuscript Bible equalled seven years' income for ordinary people, but even early printed Bibles were relatively expensive.

The standard medieval Bible was the Latin vulgate translation. St. Jerome was responsible for most of this translation, but for several books he retained or merely revised earlier Latin versions. In many passages the older Latin version pushed aside St. Jerome's translation in actual use. Copyist errors and constant revisions insured that there was no uniform version of the vulgate until printing helped to fix the text. The medieval doctor of theology devoted several years to biblical studies before turning to systematic theology. An interesting indirect evidence that educated clergymen read the Bible assiduously is the fact that many medieval writers depended for their literary effects on a thorough knowledge of the Latin Bible among their readers—for instance the letters of Peter of Blois, long popular reading, and the sermons of Jean Gerson. The humour in the Latin parody on clerical avarice, *The Gospel According to the Marks of Silver*, pivots on putting scriptural phrases to novel use; anybody who does not know the original context of the phrase will not catch the humour. The first known printed book is the Gutenberg Bible of 1455. By 1500 there were a hundred printed editions of the whole Latin Bible; small editions of the Psalms and Gospels were even more popular. Latin was, of course, the language of the medieval universities and scholarship; indeed, more books were published in Latin before the reformation than in all other languages combined.

What of the uneducated who could not read Latin? During the Middle Ages Catholics or heretics had translated the Bible into every major language of Christendom. By 1500 there were thirty printed editions of the Bible in six vernacular languages. Nevertheless, the medieval church generally opposed making vernacular translations available to laymen. Fearful over the Lollards, the English hierarchy refused to authorize any vernacular edition. The Spanish Inquisition destroyed every copy of the Catalan Bible published at Valencia in 1478. The medieval church failed to provide translations because she feared that heretics would use them to raise objections to current teaching and practice. Moreover, the hierarchy felt that the Bible was too difficult for the uneducated to understand. Typical was Innocent III who praised the desire of laymen to understand scripture but continued: "The hidden mysteries of the faith should not be opened to all without discrimination ... for so profound is the depth of scripture that not only the simple and uneducated but even the prudent and learned cannot fully explain its meaning." When the Catholic church began making translations widely available, it was mainly to counter Protestant versions. The argument that religious art provided "the Bible of the poor" carries little weight because much of the Bible cannot be pictured and because religious art, for example the windows and statues of the Gothic cathedrals, often presupposes rather than supplies an intimate knowledge of Bible history. Perhaps more effective than art in teaching Bible history were the mystery plays which were staged in every western European country. The church did allow vernacular translations of the Sunday epistles and gospels; printed copies of these became so common in the late fifteenth century that many churches replaced some of their stained glass with clear windows to provide better light for reading.

How did the Middle Ages understand the Bible? Again, no simple answer is possible. Aquinas differed from St. Bernard in using the Bible as much as Rudolf Bultmann differs from Billy Graham. The allegorical method of scripture interpretation, worked out by Origen at Alexandria and employed by most of the Greek and Latin church Fathers, shaped the approach of most medieval writers. Because they were convinced that a single meaning could not exhaust the marvelous profundity of scripture, medieval interpreters found four levels of meaning in the Bible. The literal meaning gives the facts of salvation history. The allegorical sense shows the doctrinal meaning, particularly how Old Testament men and events foreshadow the story of Christ and the church. The moral sense of scripture teaches man his sinfulness and his calling to Christian holiness. Finally the anagogic sense stresses man's eternal fate in heaven or hell. The fourfold interpretation applied best to the historical books of the Old Testament; elsewhere its use was restricted. Theoretically the allegorical approach allowed an interpreter to read into a text nearly anything he fancied, but in practice patristic authority and the clear sense of the Bible as a whole helped check the worst abuses. The best medieval exegetes, Andrew of St. Victor, Aquinas and Nicholas of Lyra, kept close to the historical and literal sense. Many scholastic theologians allowed only a literal interpretation in questions of doctrine and relegated the other senses to pious meditation or preaching. Most medieval exegetes were weak in philology and history. Thanks to the availability of Jewish rabbis as teachers, they were more likely to know Hebrew than Greek.

At the Grass Roots

The real life of the church takes place on the parish level. The vitality of parish life depended on the quality of the priest: "As the priest is, so are his people" was a favorite medieval proverb borrowed from Isaiah, but generalizations about the quality of the medieval clergy are hazardous because conditions varied and there are few reliable statistics. The lower clergy certainly were not rich. Figures for one English diocese in 1320 suggest that priests had an income about fifty percent higher than ploughmen. To raise their income many priests tried to acquire several benefices, but this increased absenteeism. Recent studies of several English dioceses around 1510 suggest an absentee rate of about fifteen percent. If the country parishes were often understaffed, the cities suffered a glut of priests. Fifteenth century Lübeck, with 350 priests for its 25,000 inhabitants, was not unusual. Most objectionable were the mass-priests who had no pastoral duties but subsisted on the stipend of a daily mass for a deceased patron. Extreme examples were fifty-four mass-priests at the cathedral of Constance and 122 at St. Elizabeth's in Breslau during the late Middle Ages. Intelligent observers argued for fewer and better priests, but effective reforms were not introduced. Only a handful of the clerical proletariate in town and country were properly trained. Perhaps five percent of the parish clergy were university educated. Most well trained priests tried to stay at the universities or sought advancement in the chanceries. According to the canon lawyers the minimum knowledge for priests—often not attained in practice—was modest enough: enough Latin to pronounce correctly and understand the literal sense of liturgical texts, the correct manner of administering the sacraments, the basic doctrines of faith, and the proper distinctions between types of sin.

Theoretically parish priests had the duty to teach children *gratis*, but they seldom taught at all, much less for free. Even catechetical instruction was quite exceptional in the Middle Ages. Parents were expected to teach their children the Creed, the Lord's Prayer and the Ten Commandments, but this was done so badly that in 1451 the Cardinal Legate to Germany ordered that wood tablets containing these basic statements be set up in the churches. The invention of printing led to an outpouring of prayerbooks, lives of the saints, manuals for confessors and preachers, guides for annual confession and the like, but the pre-reformation church published no effective catechism for children.

Boniface VIII in his controversy with Philip IV frankly admitted that "the experience of modern times clearly shows the hostility of the laity for the clergy." The rise of anti-clericalism stemmed from both subjective and objective factors. Prejudice tends to focus on any social group that differs from the majority. Like the medieval Jews, clergymen wore distinctive clothing, were governed by different laws and were exempt from many taxes and obligations. Obviously celibacy separated them from other men, and they tended to develop a subculture and distinctive life-style. Their calling obliged them to denounce the failings of other men; under the best circumstances this could arouse resentment. The moral failings of the clergy were judged by a stricter standard and opened them to charges of hypocrisy. The ignorance, indolence and poverty of the clerical proletariate bred contempt. The wealth of the higher clergy alienated many, especially when combined with the aggressiveness of the self-made man. Thus the nobility despised Cardinal Wolsey for his low birth, while commoners loathed his air of superiority. Celibacy made demands that many clerics were not prepared to meet; there are no overall statistics, but concubinage was not uncommon, especially in country parishes. Many bishops chose to look the other way or impose fines rather than energetically uproot this abuse.

Many monasteries of the late Middle Ages owned extensive lands but contributed little to society; except for the charterhouses, few were centers of intense piety or intellectual distinction. The mendicant orders also had fallen from their earlier fervor. Because the friars seldom had the endowed wealth of the monks, they had to scramble for small bequests so that they appeared petty and grasping. Again there were exceptions: the Spanish and Irish Franciscans, for example, were undergoing revivals on the eve of the reformation.

During the high Middle Ages the church had provided most of the educational and social welfare institutions of society. In the late Middle Ages these came progressively under lay control, and the church was more closely confined to spiritual and pastoral duties. To many, her wealth seemed disproportionate to her smaller role, especially since she performed her pastoral tasks so indifferently.

For centuries members of religious orders had claimed the title of religious on the grounds that their vocation was higher or more religious than the laity's. In the late Middle Ages many laymen rejected this claim: holiness depended on love for God and love for man, not on wearing cowl or coif. When a friar told St. Catherine of Genoa that his calling allowed him to love God better, she replied that if she believed she could thereby gain for herself a single spark of greater love, she would take away his habit by force.

The growth of anti-clericalism does not prove that the Catholic clergy was getting worse or that religous fervor was declining at the end of the Middle Ages. Quite the contrary. The clerical abuses were of long standing: the criticism of the clergy on the eve of the reformation by Erasmus and Sebastian Brant have earlier parallels in Boccaccio and Chaucer. There is even evidence that the quality of the clergy was improving around 1500. Certainly the educational level was rising—one recent study even concludes that about forty percent of the clergy of south Germany had studied at universities. Rather the clergy was caught up in a revolution of rising religious expectations. The laity was also better educated and would no longer tolerate ignorant, lazy or sinful priests. Perhaps never was northern Europe more God-hungry than in the late fifteenth century, especially in Germany. Roughly seventy-five percent of all books published before the reformation dealt with religious subjects. Religious art, most clearly in Hieronymus Bosch, Mathias Grünewald and Tilman Riemenschneider, often took on an unbearable intensity, especially in depicting Christ's passion.

Side by side with this intense religiosity was a lassitude about fundamental reform. In northern Europe the church produced only one major thinker during the fifteenth century, Nicholas of Cusa (1401-1464), and his writings were too esoteric to command a wide audience. Another index of Catholic vitality is the appearance of new religious orders. The last noteworthy foundation was the Brethren of the Common Life, but they were largely confined to the Netherlands and northwestern Germany in contrast to the wide diffusion of earlier orders. The founder of the Brethren was a plain Dutchman, Gerhard Groote (1340-1384), who insisted on practical piety and put little store in mystical flights or scholastic subtlety. The Brethren were not a religious order in the strict sense, for they followed no formal rule and took no vows. They lived and prayed together in small communities, but members could leave whenever they chose. Everyone was expected to work for his livelihood. At first they engaged in many manual trades, but guild opposition channeled their activities to teaching, running student hostels and especially to copying books of devotion for middle class laymen. Their practicality allowed them to get into the new printing trade with marked success.

Associated with the Brethren was the Modern Devotion movement which spread Groote's preaching that men must repent, turn to God, imitate Christ and show their devotion in active charity. The Modern Devotion produced numberless religious tracts, including the classic *Imitation of Christ* by Thomas à Kempis (1380-1471). Aside from the Bible, no book has enjoyed such lasting popularity among Christians of all denominations. Alternating pious reflections with dialogues between God and the soul, the *Imitation* urges union with God in simple, earnest words. It must have served as an antidote to the mechanical repetition of religious acts which character-ized much late medieval piety. Although intensely ethical and without a developed theology of grace, it probably also moderated the Pelagian tendencies of many nominalist theo-logians. Less admirable is its pervasive anti-intellectualism: "What will it profit you to argue learnedly about the Trinity, if you lack humility and thereby displease the Trinity?" Moreover, the spirituality of the *Imitation* lacks a social dimension. The withdrawal to cultivate God within becomes so absorbing that it disregards the Christian transformation of society. Although the *Imitation* never questions ortho-doxy, it largely ignores the institutional church.

The intense religious spirit of the late Middle Ages should not be underestimated, for it was the wellspring of both the Protestant and Catholic reformations. Nevertheless many medieval churchmen allowed the letter of canon law to govern their actions more than the Christian law of charity. They failed to measure their actions against the ideals of the early church. Even the church of the first century, as the New Testament makes clear, did not escape disagreements, here-sies and sinful Christians. While the Bible must serve as yard-stick for the church in every age, its application to the life of the church is never easy. On many questions of doctrine and conduct the Bible gives clear answers, but on many other questions that have arisen over the centuries the Bible is silent or vague. Moreover, the on-going church can never try to be a mere carbon copy of the primitive church since it must apply the Gospel to a new age and changed circumstances, nor is it easy to determine what is a distortion of the Gospel and what is legitimate adaptation. In applying the Gospel, the church is always struggling against deep-rooted inclina-tions to evil in the clergy and laity alike. She must use the Bible as her guide, confident that the Holy Spirit directs her work, but careful lest she confuse the Spirit of God with the spirit of the times. Self-critical reformation is the task of Christians in every age.

4

Reformers

The Humanist

The humanist movement began in Italy at least as early as the poet Francesco Petrarch in the mid-fourteenth century. In contrast to the essentially rural civilization of the feudal north, Italy remained a land of cities. Italians, living amid the evidence and ruins of Roman civilization, experienced Rome as a part of their past to a degree impossible for Englishmen or Germans. Classical civilization had an urban tone that appealed to the citizens of Florence, Venice, and Milan. Their precocious commercial success provided the wealth and leisure to cultivate an interest in classical literature. The empty cult of chivalry fostered in the late middle ages by the kings of France and the dukes of Burgundy found little sympathy south of the Alps. Italy even muted the soaring verticle stress of Gothic architecture; in the Gothic churches of Siena, Assisi, Orvieto and Florence the decorative elements run horizontally, and the wall frescos are far more interesting than the stained glass windows. In Italy the well rounded man needed to hone his mind on something closer to life than speculative philosophy and theology. Humanism filled the need.

Humanism cannot be defined as an interpretation of man and his place in the universe, for renaissance humanists took the most divergent views. Some glorified man and his powers, others emphasized his depravity; some championed free will, others denied it. Rather than a philosophical system, humanism was a cultural program which stressed literature, the study of classical languages, and ethics. As such humanism was not concerned with mathematics, logic, physics, metaphysics, theology, law, or medicine, although many humanists were adept in these fields. Most Italian humanists remained convinced Christians, but some such as Poggio Bracciolini and Niccolo Machiavelli allowed their enthusiasm for the pagan classics to undermine their Christian faith. Thinkers such as Marsilio Ficino and Giovanni Pico della Mirandola fused Platonism and Christianity into an unstable compound.

Only in the closing decades of the fifteenth century did the humanist movement gain strength and definition north of the Alps, where it took on a religious and reformist character. Typical was Jacques Lefèbvre d'Etaples (c. 1450-1537). Although a philosophy professor at Paris, he journeyed to Italy to study Plato with Ficino at Florence, then investigated Aristotle at Padua. On returning to France he published translations and commentaries on almost all of Aristotle's works. Nevertheless his other writings reveal an inwardness that reaches back to the medieval German mystics Meister Eckhart, Johann Tauler and Nicholas of Cusa. Lefèbvre insisted that the Bible was central to Christian thought and urged a more philological and historical approach to its study; his edition of the Psalms printed five versions in parallel columns for instant comparison. His commentary on St. Paul's epistles foreshadowed the ideas of Luther regarding faith and good works, and he translated the New Testament into French. Encouraged by the reforming bishop of Meaux, Guillaume Briçonnet, Lefèbvre and a circle of young priests tried to re-invigorate piety on the local level by a program of religious education, including broadsheets with biblical passages in simple French. The Meaux reformers emphasized intelligent personal religion at the expense of traditional practices.

They soon came under fire from the conservative theologians who dominated the University of Paris. Some of their circle became Protestants, for instance, Guillaume Farel who evangelized Geneva; but Lefèbvre and Briçonnet remained in communion with Rome.

The leading English humanist at the turn of the century was John Colet (c. 1467-1519), dean of St. Paul's Cathedral in London. Like Lefèbvre he reacted against his early training in scholastic philosophy and theology and studied neo-Platonism in Florence. His lectures at Oxford from 1496 to 1504 on the Bible caused a sensation. They presented a curious mixture of the new humanist interpretation, medieval allegory, neo-Platonic mysticism, and a somber Augustinian view of man. Man is enslaved to sin, alienated from God, and can come to grace only through scripture and divine help. His preaching influenced many, notably Thomas More and Erasmus. Colet's great confidence in education led him to devote much of his family fortune to founding St. Paul's School, modelled after Italian humanist schools which encouraged the study of classical Latin and Greek.

Very similar was the career of the German humanist Johann Reuchlin (1455-1522). At Florence he developed an uncritical enthusiasm for Hebrew studies which embraced not only the Old Testament but also the Cabala, a collection of medieval Jewish theosophical writings. His Hebrew grammar published in 1506 solidified his reputation as the leading Christian Hebraist. When a converted Jew, Pfefferkorn, and the Cologne Dominicans urged that the conversion of the Jews to Christianity would be speeded if their books were destroyed, Reuchlin countered that a knowledge of Hebrew writings such as the Talmud was indispensable for biblical studies. The German humanists flocked to defend Reuchlin and gathered their testimonials into *The Letters of Famous Men*. Several wits led by the vitriolic knight Ulrich von Hutten published *The Letters of Obscure Men*, a parody which purported to present letters in support of Pfefferkorn and his allies; in fact the letters were gross caricatures of the scholastic theologians of the day. The Pfefferkorn-Reuchlin case was eventually haled to Rome and dragged on for years. Unimportant in itself, it provided the backdrop for Luther's attack on indulgences and the counter-attack of the Dominicans. The humanists immediately acclaimed Luther as an ally, whereas Rome underestimated Luther's challenge as merely another squabble among German monks.

Desiderius Erasmus of Rotterdam (c. 1466-1536) was the acknowledged leader of the northern humanists. Although a professed Augustinian of the monastery at Steyn, he soon grew to loathe monastic life. In the monastery library he perfected a supple, aphoristic Latin style which opened the door to a larger world, first as a bishop's secretary, then as a tutor to noble boys, finally as a free lance intellectual and the literary arbiter of Christendom. Eventually he obtained a papal dispensation from his vows. Several years at the University of Paris confirmed his contempt for scholastic theology as vacuous and pompous; not only did the crabbed style of the theologians offend his literary taste, but more important he felt that scholasticism offered no nourishment for spiritual hunger, no program for the practical reform of the Church.

Gradually Erasmus came to see his life's work as the reform of the church. He called his program the philosophy of Christ and sketched its outline in *The Christian Soldier's Handbook* (1503), which enjoyed enormous popularity among educated laymen. Christianity does not consist, Erasmus argued, in external observances but in heart-felt commitment carried out in daily life. Dogma was downplayed but not discarded. His philosophy of Christ looked back to the *Imitation of Christ* and the Netherlandish *devotio moderna*, but its piety is lay rather than monastic. Like the *Imitation* it despises scholasticism, but it also stresses the contribution humanist learning can make to church reform.

For Erasmus the previous thousand years represented a

gradual perversion of Christianity by layers of encrustations and formalism. The church must renew itself by going back to its sources, the Bible and the church Fathers. Education was the key. If men could be brought into contact with authentic Christianity through the writings of the early church, they would try to recapture its spirit. Erasmus devoted the last thirty years of his life mainly to editing and publishing these writings. For scholars he published the first Greek New Testament in 1516 and added a polished Latin translation. He urged translations into all the languages of Europe so that ploughmen and housewives might discover Christ for themselves. He wrote paraphrases and commentaries on most of the Bible and produced massive editions of the church Fathers, particularly Jerome, Augustine, and Chrysostom.

Since pagans such as Plato and Seneca taught many sound moral principles which Christianity crowned and completed, the classics had a prominent place in Erasmus' plan to re-educate Christendom. Tirelessly he wrote text books for almost every level of renaissance education: Latin phrasebooks, sample dialogues, compilations of quotations, directions on how to write letters. These were not neutral exercise books—shot through them all was the philosophy of Christ. His towering reputation and the favor of many high churchmen protected Erasmus from counter-attack. With his chosen weapon, the rapier of satire, he was invincible; and enemies found themselves destroyed by a clever phrase or telling aphorism. Erasmus soon had the educated of Europe laughing with him. His masterpiece, *The Praise of Folly*, combines humor and seriousness and mocks the foibles of all classes and occupations, but especially the clergy. The early generations of the reformation era were brought up on his books.

"Right now I almost wish I were young again for this reason alone, that I foresee a golden age coming on," wrote Erasmus in February 1517 to his friend Wolfgang Capito. "I anticipate with certainty that morality and Christian holiness together with reforms, good order, and purer literature shall gain in vitality and splendor, especially because (the rulers) of the various countries are giving their support with equal energy." Little did Erasmus realize that within a year humanism would be overtaken by a far more dynamic movement, and that Capito and many of his friends would soon be following a new leader, Martin Luther. The writings of Erasmus prepared many for Luther's message. Later critics accused Erasmus of laying the egg that Luther hatched, but Erasmus had no desire to overturn the church; he aimed at gradual moral and institutional reform from within. He was dismayed by Luther's insistence on man's total depravity and his break with the hierarchical church. He frankly told Luther, "Neither death nor life shall draw me from the communion of the Catholic church. I bear with this church, until I shall see a better, and it cannot help bearing with me until I shall be better."

Luther's preaching caused a crisis among the humanists. They shared many of the same enemies with Luther, and he had their sympathy at first. But his message was more intense and more profound. His earthy German spoke to the common man with an urgency that humanists with their elitist mentality could never command. Luther called for action and violent change, if need be, in the church. Erasmus, Reuchlin, Lefèbvre and many of the older humanists hung back after they saw the implications of Luther's message; but many of the younger humanists—Zwingli, Capito, Bucer, and Calvin— accepted it and then gradually modified it, each in his own way. When Bucer asked him why he had not thrown in his lot with the Protestants, Erasmus replied that he was dismayed over their quarreling. "I seem to see a cruel and bloody century ahead. Those who have abandoned the Hours do not pray at all. Those who disdain episcopal regulations do not even obey God's commandments."

Martin Luther
Martin Luther, the most important figure in Christian his-

tory since St. Paul, was born in 1483 at Eisleben in central Germany. He spent his youth in nearby Mansfeld, where his father prospered in the mining business. Luther completed his education at the large, conservative University of Erfurt, where he studied Aristotle and developed a vigorous Latin style. He read widely in the Latin classics, particularly the poets, and was fond of quoting them throughout his life. Perhaps he loved the poets too much, for he ranked thirtieth in a class of fifty-two when he took his bachelor's degree. He advanced to second of seventeen when he graduated as a master of arts. His proud father presented him with a book of Roman law; Luther accepted the suggestion and entered the law school. Two months later he abruptly invited his friends to a party and gave away most of his books. The next day Martin entered the strict Augustinian monastery at Erfurt. Hans Luther was furious, for he expected a lucrative career for his son.

Luther's decision was not as abrupt as it seemed. The monastic life was the surest road to heaven in the medieval view, and Erfurt was filled with art and other reminders which underlined the awful seriousness of the human condition poised between heaven and hell. Luther himself had undergone two recent brushes with death that reinforced the lesson. Luther spent a year of novitiate in spiritual training before he took perpetual vows of poverty, chastity, and obedience. The next year, 1507, he was ordained and celebrated his first mass.

After five years of further study Luther was awarded the doctorate in theology and assumed the chair of biblical studies at the new University of Wittenberg. His studies rested on the writings of Gabriel Biel, a nominalist who stressed God's mysterious power. Reason cannot plumb the nature of God, and man should not lean on the weak reed of philosophy. Rather the Christian must accept the teaching of the Bible as explained by the church in its dogmas. If man strives to do his best, God will not deny him grace; with this grace man can increase his merit in God's eyes and confidently await his reward in heaven. Luther memorized long passages from Biel's *Commentary on the Canon of the Mass* which attempted to give a practical, pastoral slant to nominalism, but his teaching brought Luther no peace of heart. Luther was prayerful and austere, but his efforts could not silence the questions that kept welling up: "Am I doing enough? Do I possess God's favor? Are my sins forgiven? How can I be sure of salvation?" He redoubled his prayer and penances, but the questions continued. Again and again he confessed his sins and doubts to his superior, Johann Staupitz, who tried to comfort the young professor: trust in God's forgiving love, trust in the merits of Christ. But how can man trust? On what basis? God commands that men love him with the whole heart and the whole soul. Who can fulfill that awful command? God appeared to Luther as an arbitrary tyrant, as stern and implacable as his father Hans.

Luther continued to search the scriptures for an answer to his gnawing problem. Then the answer came. Late in life Luther described it as a sudden breakthrough, perhaps telescoping a more gradual process. Scholars today debate the exact year. Luther was reflecting in the monastery tower on the meaning of St. Paul's statement (Rom. 1:17): "For in the Gospel the justice of God is revealed through faith for faith, 'for he shall live who is justified by faith.'" Previously Luther had seen the justice of God as active, as judging man and holding him to account. Now he saw this justice as passive— God freely credits the man of faith with righteousness because of Christ's merits. Luther's discovery of a gracious God who justifies by faith alone brought him peace. "Then I grasped that the justice of God is the righteousness by which, through grace and pure mercy, God justifies us through faith. Instantly I knew that I had been reborn and had entered paradise through an open door!" The faith that saves was no mere intellectual assent but a casting of the whole self, naked and helpless, upon God's mercy, a clinging to Christ crucified who alone delivers man from his corruption.

Justification through faith alone proved the fundamental doctrine on which the Protestant reformation rests. Using it as a criterion Luther gradually came to reassess the whole medieval program of salvation. As he began to work the new viewpoint into his lectures, they grew in clarity, confidence and popularity. His study of St. Augustine confirmed his belief, and convinced him that many medieval practices and most scholastic theologians were shot through with the same Pelagianism that Augustine had refuted centuries earlier. Luther rejected the notion that grace was a power that God poured into men to make them just. On the contrary, man remains a sinner in all his actions, for he can never perfectly fulfill the commandment to love God with the whole heart; in view of this commandment, all man's actions are sinful. Nevertheless, the man of faith, while remaining sinful, is justified because God does not count his sins against him but clothes him in Christ's righteousness. Good works do not justify men, but the just man performs good works as the fruit and sign of his justification. Moreover, man cannot contribute to his justification because original sin inherited from Adam has clouded his reason, stripped him of his freedom and drives him ever toward sin. In the face of God's infinite power and knowledge of all future actions, human freedom is an empty boast.

Luther continually urged both God's all-powerful majesty and his gracious dealing with man. He saw little value in philosophical concepts about God derived from Aristotle. The God who is pure act and self-subsistent being is a construct of the scholastics, remote and irrelevant to man. The God whom Luther experienced in his anguish and found in the Bible was both closer to man and more majestic. The Bible describes His acts in history and His plan to save men. Every contingent act of man and of nature exists solely because He wills it. Yet this awesome, hidden God stands ever present, sustaining and gracious, in the page of scripture, in prayer, in the tide of daily activity, in the crisis of temptation. This God became man, endured human pain, suffered human death and has now risen as the first born of the new creation. On the eve of the reformation Germans were God-obsessed and God-starved. Luther preached a God they could trust, who could satisfy their hunger.

Luther's transformation from young professor at a provincial university to a figure of world historical importance was accidental and meteoric. Near Wittenberg in October 1517 the Dominican Johann Tetzel began preaching an indulgence to raise money for the building of St. Peter's basilica in Rome. For several centuries the papacy had encouraged specific good works, including contributions to the building of churches, by attaching to them a share in the merits of Christ and the saints. An indulgence was considered effective only if the indulgence seeker sincerely repented and confessed his serious sins. The theologians tried to hedge the theory of indulgences with safeguards but high pressure salesmen like Tetzel often quietly dropped them. To the populace grace and salvation seemed up for sale at discount prices. Luther felt it his duty as a theologian to protest, so he wrote ninety-five theses discussing indulgences which he proposed to defend publicly. Such public disputations were ordinary academic procedures. Scholars argue whether Luther actually nailed them to the church door which served as the university bulletin board. Most of the theses were acceptable enough in Catholic theology, but their wording was provocative. Copies were sold everywhere and caused a sensation; to his surprise Luther found himself a national hero who opposed easy salvation and the drain of hard-earned German gold to Rome. Some writers attacked him, some rallied to his defense; others such as Erasmus kept silent and awaited developments.

Luther was his own best defender in bold, slashing pamphlets. Gradually the issues under debate opened out and the sweeping revision of medieval thought and practice implicit in the doctrine of justification through faith alone stood revealed. Among the best of Luther's four hundred tracts and pamphlets were two that appeared in 1520. *The Babylonian Captivity of the Church*, which was addressed in Latin to theologians everywhere, subjected the Catholic sacramental system to scathing fire. Luther accepted only baptism, the eucharist, and penance as instituted by Christ. Even these were perverted in practice. The cup was kept from the layman, the ceremony was in Latin and overlaid with accretions that blocked understanding. More fundamental, the mass was not a sacrifice and the eucharistic doctrine of transubstantiation rested on metaphysical claptrap, although Luther insisted that Christ's body was really present in, with, and under the bread and wine. More slashing was the *Address to the Christian Nobility of the German Nation*, which urged the princes to throw off the yoke of Rome. A wide array of abuses—social, political, and academic—were denounced. Luther did not hesitate to appeal to German national feeling and the financial interests of the nobles and burghers, many of whom became his strongest supporters. He wholly rejected the papacy, for not only had the popes usurped both secular and spiritual power to the detriment of the church, but they were indeed the mysterious Anti-Christ described in the Bible. Luther never wavered in this conviction; his last major treatise was *Against the Papacy at Rome Founded by the Devil* (1545).

Why did Luther succeed where Waldo, Wycliffe, and Hus failed? Doubtless Luther was a greater theologian and more attractive personality, and political conditions favored him, but the printing press was a new and potent factor. By 1520 some 300,000 copies of his writings were in print. Booksellers could hardly keep up with the demand. Luther was the most influential thinker of the sixteenth century because he was its most popular and prolific writer. The Protestant reformation was the first religious movement that could multiply its message to a mass audience. The printing press gave Luther a lever to move society that offset the institutional weight of the Catholic church. Luther called printing "God's highest and ultimate act of grace which drives forward the work of the Gospel."

Luther's enemies promptly instituted heresy charges against him, and for several years there were complex negotiations between papal representatives, Luther, and Frederick the Wise of Saxony, who supported Luther. There were public debates as well, most notably at Leipzig in June and July, 1519. The Catholic Johann Eck, a skilled debater with a prodigious memory and stentorian voice, easily got the best of Andreas Carlstadt until Luther came to Carlstadt's support. The debate first treated papal authority, which Luther readily rejected, but when accused of supporting doctrines condemned at the Council of Constance, Luther went on and insisted that even ecumenical councils had erred. Scripture alone is the norm of faith.

This was a momentous step, for with it Luther undercut the teaching authority of the hierarchical church and the established rules of theology. The teaching of popes and councils now would have to be checked against scripture, and the Christian need accept no doctrine unless its scriptural foundation was clear. Luther equally rejected the Catholic theory of tradition, that there were doctrines and practices which go back to the teaching of Christ and the Apostles, or at least to the early church, which Chrsitians must accept and preserve even if they are not found explicitly in scripture. For Luther and his young colleague Philip Melanchthon this did not mean that ancient traditions and practices should be rejected. Anything contrary to scripture must indeed be ruthlessly weeded out, but there were many adiaphora, things indifferent in themselves, which the church could retain or discard as the pastoral needs of peoples and circumstances suggested. Luther was inclined to be conservative in this area. He raised no objections to priestly vestments or most of the religious art and music of the day. Some of his writings show a tender devotion to the Virgin Mary. Many medieval feast days were retained, and bishops have continued until today to direct Lutheran churches in Scandinavia, although the understanding of their function changed. Many later Protestants, especially Zwingli and the Puritans, insisted on a more drastic purging of non-scriptural practices.

Scripture alone as the norm of religious teaching had further implications. Luther was distrustful of appeals to the Holy Spirit or an inner light unless these could be buttressed from the text of scripture. Otherwise the door was open to subjectivism, wild enthusiasm, and self-deception. Luther could deal harshly with those who made claims which they could not back up with biblical texts. To be sure, the Holy Spirit working within the heart opened the meaning of God's written word, but theological argument must rest on the careful, literal exposition of the text by the best tools that history and language study could afford. Luther himself was a fine Greek scholar and competent in Hebrew.

Although Luther felt that all Christians should read the Bible in their own language, he did not believe in private interpretation of the Bible as a principle. He did not grant individuals the right to work out their own beliefs from a personal reading of the Bible; rather, the meaning of scripture is one, clear, and consistent. Certainly there are obscure passages, but these must be understood in the light of clearer passages. Luther was convinced that his own theology reflected the clear thrust of scripture and that his rejection of the teaching authority of the hierarchy did not entail doctrinal diversity and anarchy.

In June 1520 Rome replied to Luther with the Bull *Exsurge Domine* which condemned forty-one statements taken from a wide range of Luther's writings. On December 10 the students at Wittenberg built a bonfire; amid cheers Luther strode forward and threw the Bull into the flames, and the students added books of canon law and scholastic theology.

According to medieval theory, it was the task of Emperor Charles V to move against the condemned heretic. The following April Luther appeared before the Diet or parliament of the Empire convened at Worms. The Emperor's spokesman asked him to recant his teaching. Luther's answer was decisive: "Unless I am convinced by the testimony of scripture or by clear reason...my conscience is captive to the word of God. I cannot and will not retract anything since going against conscience is neither safe nor right." As he left, Luther raised his hand as a sign of victory. Charles V muttered, "He will not make me a heretic!" Luther had now defied both church and state. As an excommunicated outlaw, he could be seized at will as soon as his safe conduct from Worms expired. Burning at the stake was the punishment for heresy.

As Luther rode back to Wittenberg, a group of knights ambushed his party. Luther's companions scattered. The knights quickly disappeared into the forest. Luther was gone too, vanished from the face of the earth, perhaps murdered, or so people thought. In fact the knights were trusty servants of Frederick the Wise, who whisked Luther to safekeeping at the Wartburg Castle where Luther grew a beard, donned knight's clothes and called himself Knight George. To ease his restlessness at the Wartburg, Luther went to work on his New Testament translation. Later he spent many years polishing his work and adding the Old Testament. The result was one of the great Bible translations of all time, painstakingly capturing the precise shade of the original in vivid German. His translation did more than any other book to fix the German language during its formative era.

While Luther worked at the Wartburg, unsettling events took place at Wittenburg. Carlstadt began drastic liturgical changes; others destroyed pictures and the altars in the churches. A group of radical prophets who claimed to be inspired by the Holy Spirit arrived and demanded sweeping social changes. The people were so confused and dispirited that the town council begged Luther to return from his refuge. He arrived on March 6, 1522, and preached a series of sermons on the need for moderation and for gradual, constructive change. The town settled down and expelled the radicals. Luther resumed his teaching duties and supervised the introduction of a new liturgy. Luther composed many hymns of strength and beauty for Lutheran congregations, including the still popular "A Mighty Fortress Is Our God." He continued to live in the monastery after most of the other monks had followed his advice and married. Luther did not wed until 1525; the marriage proved fruitful and affectionate—Luther claimed he would not barter his "Empress Cathy for France or Venice."

The years after Luther's return to Wittenberg brought troubles as well as joys. Discontent had been percolating among the peasants for decades, for many feudal obligations still bore heavily on the German peasants long after their disappearance in England, France and Italy. The peasants also opposed the introduction of Roman civil law. For them Luther's emphasis on Christian freedom had an exhilarating effect. Luther meant both the freedom from Rome and the release that the conviction of justification through faith alone brought the conscience; many peasants extended his meaning to embrace social freedoms and economic rights. After wandering prophets stirred up the countryside, unco-ordinated revolts flared up through south and central Germany from 1524 to mid-1526. Where the peasants formulated their demands, as in the Swabian Twelve Articles, they often were moderate requests for specific economic and social rights; indeed, several articles insisted on a return to the old customs and laws and asked Luther to serve as arbitrator. But soon violence bred violence. Castles were razed, monasteries and towns sacked, and prisoners slaughtered. Thomas Müntzer urged on the peasants: "Don't let the blood cool on your swords." He promised divine help. Instead the armies of the princes returned from campaigning in Italy and hacked the unorganized peasants to pieces. Müntzer was caught, tried, and beheaded. Luther was sympathetic to many of the

peasants' goals but opposed the use of force against constituted authority. Only the state, he argued, has the power of
the sword and that power comes from God. Disgusted by the
peasants' violence and pillage, he wrote *Against the Robbing
and Murderous Peasant Bands* in 1526, which exhorted the
princes to "strike, strangle and stab" the rebels like mad dogs.
The princes needed no encouragement as they crushed the
peasants and imposed harsher conditions than ever. In many
areas touched by the revolt spontaneous enthusiasm for
Luther waned among the peasants; a few returned to Catholicism, while others gave ear to the new Anabaptist preachers.
Most simply accepted the religious decisions of their princes
who henceforward controlled the growth and consolidation
of the reformation in Germany.

Ulrich Zwingli

By the end of the middle ages the Swiss cantons had gained
virtual independence from the Holy Roman Empire and had
grouped themselves into a loose Confederation. Erasmian
humanism was widespread among educated priests, and
Luther's message and example galvanized many of them into
action. In Basel, Bern, St. Gall and elsewhere humanist
priests became Protestant reformers, but the center of the
Swiss reformation was Zurich and Zwingli was its leader.

Ulrich Zwingli (1481-1531) came from an Alpine village,
but his parents were prosperous enough to send him to the
Universities of Vienna and Basel. In 1506 Zwingli earned his
master of arts degree and accepted ordination. His pastoral
responsibilities were light and he devoted himself to the study
of Greek, Hebrew, neo-Platonic philosophy, and the writings
of Erasmus, with whom he corresponded. In the previous
decades the Swiss had won an enormous reputation as mercenary soldiers, and their fierce pikemen were everywhere in
demand, especially for the Italian wars. Zwingli served as
chaplain during their great victory at Novara and their disaster at Marignano. The experience left him shaken and he

criticized the mercenary system in two pamphlets which reveal a strong strain of Swiss patriotism. His powerful preaching against selling blood for gold and other abuses earned him a reputation, and in 1519 he won the coveted post of preacher at the Great Minster of Zurich. Gradually his preaching turned against fasting, confession, the mass, religious art and music, monasticism, and celibacy. Zwingli found priestly celibacy hard. He had fallen several times earlier, and as he found no such obligation in scripture, he secretly wed. His preaching carried with him most of the people of Zurich, especially the important burghers who controlled the town council.

Supported by the council, Zwingli insisted upon a public discussion on sixty-seven points at issue with the Catholics. When the bishop's representatives refused to debate or to recognize the power of the town council in religious matters, the council disregarded them and declared for Zwingli and his associates. Local monasteries were closed down and their resources allocated for charity and education. A civil court took over moral and marriage cases. The Catholic mass was forbidden, and Zwingli wrote a simplified worship service. Zwingli swept away much of medieval piety that Luther was willing to retain. Vestments disappeared, the church walls were whitewashed, and hymns were abolished, even though Zwingli was an accomplished musician with a fine singing voice. Nothing must compete with the centrality of the Word, whether preached or read from the Bible. Perhaps because of his background in humanism with its emphasis on moral reform, sacraments were far less important for Zwingli than for Luther, yet ironically controversies over the sacraments bedevilled the rest of Zwingli's life, and his followers were soon nicknamed the Sacramentarians by their enemies.

Zwingli developed his ideas about Christ's presence in the eucharist in the heat of controversy against Catholics and Lutherans. Zwingli's thought went through several stages; he and his supporters in some of their writings taught that

Christ was present in the eucharist only symbolically, just as Switzerland is symbolically present in the Swiss flag. When Christ said over the bread at the Last Supper, "This is my body," he meant that the bread remains bread but represents and symbolizes how Christ feeds by his grace the spiritual hunger and needs of his faithful. Christ's statement is a figure of speech which should not be taken literally. Much more than Luther, Zwingli generally took a rationalist, philosophical approach to theology, especially in his *On Providence*. He was reluctant to see the sacraments as objective means of grace. His symbolic teaching on the eucharist was part of this general thrust and presented a clear, logical doctrine that did away with mystery. His critics charged that dissolving mystery is not always good theology, that the New Testament eucharistic texts have a mysterious aura, and that a purely symbolic eucharist could not ground a strong liturgical tradition. Luther and Zwingli exchanged bitter tracts on the eucharist, while several theologians in the south German cities led by Martin Bucer tried to find a middle ground between Luther's real physical presence and Zwingli's symbolism.

Since the dissention weakened the Protestant cause, the most energetic of the Lutheran princes, Landgrave Philip of Hesse, tried to effect an agreement. He brought together Luther, Zwingli, and their leading supporters for a theological summit conference at his castle overlooking Marburg during October 1529. The draft proposal contained fifteen points, and on fourteen there was quick agreement; the fifteenth dealt with the eucharist, and here Luther and Zwingli agreed in condemning Catholic transubstantiation and the mass as a sacrifice, but the nature of Christ's presence proved a stumbling block. Luther began by chalking on the conference table "This is my body" lest rhetorical analysis and philosophical argument dissolve away Christ's blunt statement. For hours the discussion turned on the meaning of these four ordinary, seemingly simple words of Christ. Both sides were subtle, earnest, and sometimes passionate. At the outset Luther and Zwingli were rather contemptuous of each other, but as the argument continued they grew to respect the other's learning and sincerity. But they could not agree on the crucial point. At the end of the conference Zwingli offered his hand to Luther; it was refused, for Luther felt he could not accept the gesture in conscience. Perhaps Protestant denominationalism can be dated from that day. The meaning of the Bible was not as clear to men of learning and sincerity as Luther had assumed. The controversy on the eucharist continues today.

Zwingli also became involved in a controversy over baptism which had momentous importance. Many at Zurich felt that Zwingli and the town council were too cautious in their reforms. Led by the wealthy humanist Conrad Grebel and the former priest George Blaurock, they gathered in homes for prayer and Bible discussions which centered on the relation of the faithful to civil society. For both Luther and Zwingli the state and the religious community were co-extensive in their membership. Man was born into the one and immediately baptized into the other. Grebel and Blaurock found no authorization for this in scripture. The church should be a gathered community of believers who had committed themselves to Christian living and had covenanted themselves to brotherhood with their crucified Saviour. Membership in such a church could not be open to all members of civil society since many men were ungodly.

Entrance into this gathered community was through adult baptism, which consecrated not merely the Christian's act of belief but also his repentance for past sinfulness and his personal determination to live out the full Gospel. Infants were clearly unable to make such a commitment. On January 21, 1525, Grebel baptized Blaurock and other baptisms followed. Anabaptism was born. Like many other religious titles (Jesuits, Quakers, Methodists) *Anabaptism* was coined in derision, for the word means rebaptism. Of course the

Anabaptists rejected the implication, because in their eyes infant baptism was only a sham. The Anabaptists were unimpressed by the arguments of Zwingli and the other reformers that just as circumcision initiated infants into the covenanted community of the Old Testament, so baptism was valid for infants. There is no clear instance of infant baptism in the New Testament, although the baptism of whole households is mentioned.

When the Anabaptists continued to preach and win converts, especially among the lower classes, the town council with Zwingli's approval arrested their leaders and banished several of them. Undaunted, they continued their preaching; many were martyred in both the Catholic and Protestant cantons. The courage of the martyrs impressed observers and won many converts. In German speaking lands, the Anabaptists could count more martyrs than Catholics, Lutherans, and Calvinists combined.

Most of the Anabaptist preachers were gentle and earnest men who accepted the danger of their calling as a bond with Christ crucified, but some preached in a militant, apocalyptic tone. Melchior Hofmann denounced Luther as a Judas and proclaimed himself as the Apostle of the Last Days, which he predicted would come in 1533. His message won many converts in the Netherlands. At Münster in northwest Germany the Anabaptists gradually gained control of the city government. This first political success proved to be a disaster for the movement. Radical Dutch converts flooded into Münster and established a theocratic reign of terror which included polygamy and the common ownership of property. All books save the Bible were burned. The radical Jan of Leiden set himself up as the King of New Jerusalem with fifteen wives, splendid clothes, pompous ceremonial and vicious bodyguards. He divided the earth among his followers. Meanwhile a Catholic-Lutheran army beseiged the town and the people slowly starved. Jan promised deliverance by Easter of 1534 but neither earthly nor angelic hosts came to the rescue. When the city fell in June, many of the Anabaptists were butchered out of hand. Jan was paraded around northern Germany on a chain, then picked to death by red hot tongs.

The Münster debacle increased the persecutions since Anabaptists seemed a threat to civil order and public morality. New leaders, especially Menno Simons, saved what they could of the movement by purging the radicals. Simons insisted that the church was a free gathering of Christians who followed Christ by deeds; although warfare and government service were forbidden believers, Christians must obey the secular state in everything not contrary to scripture. His followers, the Mennonites, quietly flourished in the Netherlands and northern Germany and today number about half a million around the world. Struck by the voluntary communism of the earliest Christians, Jacob Hutter gathered other Anabaptists into voluntary, collectivist communities in eastern Europe where persecution was only sporadic. There were about eighty such Hutterite communities, each with about two hundred members, mainly skilled farmers. Centuries later many Hutterites emigrated to North and South America where they continue the old communal life-style in the twentieth century.

Nowhere except at Rome itself where church and state so closely linked together as in Zurich. Theoretically the town council took over complete direction of church matters, including doctrine; in fact Zwingli's moral ascendancy over the council was so great that the real initiative was his. He even took the lead in diplomatic affairs. Encouraged by Philip of Hesse he attempted to weave a vast alliance against the Catholic Swiss cantons and their Austrian allies. The alliance was to include the Protestant cantons, the Luthern princes and towns of the Empire, and Zwingli even hoped to win over the Catholic enemies of Hapsburg hegemony, France and Venice. His aims were an explosive mixture of religion and politics. He wanted to protect and increase

Zurich's territory but also to extend his reformation into the Catholic cantons of the Swiss Confederacy. At first his policy seemed successful, but the breakdown of the Marburg discussions alienated the Lutherans. Even though the powerful Protestant canton of Bern hung back, Zwingli pressed a blockade against the Catholic forest cantons. This threatened not only their faith and their position in the Confederation, but their very livelihood. In a desperate mood eight thousand of them crossed the Zurich border; outnumbered and unprepared, the Zurichers came out to meet them with Zwingli at their head, sword in hand. The battle at Kappel, October 11, 1531, proved a disaster which cost many of Zurich's leaders, including Zwingli, their lives. The peace of Kappel was a compromise which allowed both faiths in Switzerland. Zwingli's death held a double irony since his first fame stemmed from his preaching against mercenary war, yet the battle marked the beginning of the long history of Swiss neutrality, and the land of mercenaries became the land of bankers and watchmakers.

John Calvin

John Calvin was born in 1509 at Noyon in northern France. Coming a full generation after Luther and Zwingli, he contributed few new ideas to the Protestant reformation, but his genius for organization was precisely what Protestantism needed as Roman Catholicism began to regather its immense latent strength.

Calvin's personality contrasts strongly with Luther's warmth and volubility. Calvin was severe and self-contained except for sudden bursts of anger which he regretted and strove to overcome. Luther enjoyed good health much of his life, whereas Calvin was wracked by insomnia, migraine, hemorrhoids, kidney stones, and tuberculosis; still his dauntless spirit drove his frail body to exhaustion in his ministry. Luther's training centered on scholastic theology, while Calvin was an accomplished humanist before he turned to theology.

Calvin's father was notary to the diocese of Noyon and obtained a benefice for his eleven year old son, who was at first destined for the priesthood. Calvin studied at Paris from 1523 to 1527, but when both his priest-brother and his father fell under excommunication, Calvin abandoned an ecclesiastical career and began to study law at Orléans and Bourges. Privately he continued his humanistic interest and published an erudite commentary on the Stoic philosopher Seneca. Although only twenty-three and personally shy, Calvin was so conscious of his intellectual gifts that his commentary did not hesitate to criticize Erasmus; indeed Calvin even sent Erasmus a copy!

The commentary reveals no inclination toward the Protestant ideas which were circulating rather freely among the younger French intellectuals despite the fulminations of the theology faculty at the Sorbonne. Several of Calvin's friends accepted these ideas and urged them on him, but the transition from humanism to Protestantism was not so easy for the young Frenchman as it had been for Zwingli. Later he wrote that "I remained obstinately devoted to the superstitions of the papacy." Sometime late in 1533 Calvin underwent a sudden conversion which he attributed directly to God. A sermon by his Protestant friend Nicholas Cop cast suspicion on Calvin and forced him to leave Paris for southern France.

Shortly thereafter the condition of French Protestants changed dramatically. Francis I, a shallow profligate who fancied himself the patron of humanism and progress, had restricted persecution to sporadic outbursts. On the morning of October 18, 1534, Parisians woke up to find the city plastered with placards which ridiculed Catholic teaching. One was affixed to the door of the royal bedchamber, and the King found another in the place where he kept his handkerchiefs. A vast conspiracy seemed afoot which could reach unseen right into the royal chambers. Francis was furious and all France with him. The reaction was savage. The King ordered solemn ceremonies of expiation for the blasphemies, climaxed by the burning of six Protestants. Other executions followed. Calvin wisely fled to Basel in Switzerland, where he continued to study theology and write.

In 1536 he published the fruit of his reflection, *The Institutes of the Christian Religion.* The first Basel edition was hardly longer than a catechism, but every few years until 1559 Calvin revised his masterwork, and each edition grew thicker as Calvin added new sections and arguments distilled from his pastoral experience and polemics. Intended as an introduction to the Bible and a compendium of theology, the *Institutes* contains four books. The first deals with man's knowledge of God, scripture and creation. The next takes up Adam's sin, its crippling effects on mankind, and God's plan to save men by the redeeming life, death and resurrection of Christ. The third book describes the life of the Christian under the influence of the Holy Spirit. The final book examines the church and its membership, organization, ministries and sacraments. The *Institutes* stands unmatched in early Protestant thought for its combination of clarity, elegance, force and comprehensive scope.

The *Institutes* was Calvin's greatest book, but his greatest accomplishment was the transformation of Geneva into what John Knox called the "most perfect school of Jesus Christ since the Apostles." In the fifteenth century Geneva had a reputation for loose morals, and its initial decision to become Protestant perhaps owed more to a desire to undercut the political power of its bishop and the Dukes of Savoy than to a thirst for pure doctrine and conduct. In his dying remarks to his fellow pastors Calvin insisted that when he arrived in Geneva no real reformation had taken place, only preaching, rioting, and the destruction of religious statues.

Curiously Calvin never liked the Genevans, whom he termed a "wicked and perverse nation." He would much have preferred a life of scholarship, meditation and writing, and his ministry at Geneva came by accident. While passing through the city in 1536 he was recognized as the brilliant young author of the *Institutes* by Guillaume Farel, the firebrand reformer of Geneva. Farel, who needed help to keep the city from slipping into religious anarchy or Catholicism, insisted that Calvin remain in Geneva and called down a divine curse on his desire for scholarly leisure. Calvin was so shaken that he agreed to take up the ministry at Geneva as a direct call from God.

Calvin has been called the theocrat and spiritual dictator of Geneva. This is misleading. He was often at loggerheads with the town government. In April 1538 Farel and Calvin were even forced to leave Geneva because they refused to accept certain minor liturgical regulations of the town government. Calvin went to Strasbourg where he served as pastor to the French church. There he had an opportunity to examine and discuss the ideas and pastoral experiments of Martin Bucer, the dynamic reformer of the city. His later work in Geneva was greatly indebted to Bucer. Calvin's opponents at Geneva proved politically inept, and his friends carried the 1541 city elections. He was welcomed back and resided in Geneva until his death in 1564. Even then his leadership did not go unchallenged. Politicians opposed the church's claim to exercise excommunication, and many old Genevans resented the influx of Huguenot refugees. Geneva depended on Bern for protection, and there was no love lost between Calvin and the Bernese. More serious were the theological challenges.

Jerome Bolsec was a former Carmelite who accepted all of Calvin's teaching except the doctrine that God directly predestines some men to hell regardless of their sins or virtues. In 1551 he arose at a meeting of the local ministers and argued that Calvin's doctrine makes God a tyrant and the author of sin. Calvin replied on the spot with a torrent of passages from scripture and St. Augustine, and Bolsec was arrested after the meeting. All the Geneva pastors ratified Calvin's teaching, but he was sorely disappointed when the other Swiss churches hesitated to endorse it. Despite considerable sympathy among the citizens, Bolsec was banished for life; many years later he took revenge by writing a hostile biography of Calvin.

On the balance the Bolsec affair undermined Calvin's influence, but four years later a new controversy provided him with his greatest triumph. Michael Servetus, a learned Aragonese physician, had long harbored doubts about the doctrine of the Trinity, in which he saw a stumbling block to the conversion of Jews and Moslems. He attacked the Trinity in two books; his own views on Christ were a curious blend of theosophy, apocalyptic speculation, and ideas condemned by the early church councils. He was imprisoned by the Inquisition at Catholic Vienne but escaped and went to Geneva, where Calvin demanded his arrest. His answers to interrogation profoundly shocked the city officials. He even insisted that Calvin was the heretic, demanded his exile, and laid claim to Calvin's goods. His arrogance alienated any potential support, and Calvin's friends and enemies vied in attacking him. The other Protestant towns of Switzerland demanded his execution. Calvin urged the death penalty but disapproved of burning as too barbarous. The government brushed aside his suggestions, and Servetus went to his death proclaiming his belief even as the flames engulfed him. Later several Italian refugees at Geneva also developed anti-trinitarian views; they were exiled to Poland where they planted the seeds of later Unitarianism.

Servetus made Calvin a town hero. In the years following the trial many fervent French disciples gained citizenship, and Calvin's Genevan enemies either left town in disgust or were exiled. During the last decade of his life Calvin dominated Geneva, but his ascendance rested on his prestige, intelligence, and hard work rather than any political power.

After his return from Strasbourg in 1541 Calvin drew up the *Ecclesiastical Ordinances* as a sort of constitution for the Geneva church. The church was distinct from the city government, although there was no separation of church and state. There were still areas of friction, especially over the church's right to discipline and excommunicate for moral lapses. The *Ordinances* specify four church offices, those of doctor, pastor, elder, and deacon. The doctors, headed by

Calvin himself, taught theology. Eventually the Academy at Geneva grew to three hundred students from all over Europe, many of whom were preparing for the ministry. The pastors ran the eight city parishes. Preaching was their main task, and long sermons dominated the service, not just on Sunday but on Monday, Wednesday, and Friday as well. Calvin wanted a communion service at least monthly, but the government restricted it to four times a year. There were also ten parishes in the country-side under Genevan control, which were often used as training ground for the young ministers being prepared for missionary work. From 1555 to 1562 the tiny Geneva church sent out one hundred ministers on missions, most to France and many to martyrdom.

For Calvin an essential characteristic of the true church was discipline, and his efforts to control belief and morals through the consistory became the most controversial part of his legacy. The consistory consisted of five ministers, including Calvin, and twelve lay elders who were approved by the city government. Morals courts were common in the sixteenth century; Geneva was unique only in the thoroughness and fairness of its courts. The discipline it imposed could be picayune: missing services, laughing during sermons, owning love stories, saying the Pope was a good man, all brought down the consistory's wrath. Nobody was exempt—Calvin's own sister-in-law fell into adultery several times and was remanded to the government for further punishment. Once the consistory even censured its own president for dancing at a wedding; he took his punishment humbly and remained Calvin's good friend. The usual punishment was public humiliation or a tongue lashing, which Calvin developed into a fine art. More serious crimes were turned over to the civil courts. During Calvin's years in Geneva the population ran about 12,000 and executions averaged six per year. Justice was certainly severe, but Geneva's criminal codes were no more draconian that elsewhere, although their enforcement was more efficient.

Strange to say, there were even complaints that the courts worked too fast!

The deacons were Calvin's fourth ministry, and they carried the main responsibility for the church's social action. As in many other cities, the reformation at Geneva speeded up a process of secularization and rationalization of the local institutions for charity and welfare. Shortly before Calvin's arrival eight welfare organizations and their funds were consolidated into the General Hospital. The directors of the Hospital were elected by the city government, but Calvin consecrated their activities by identifying them with the New Testament title and office of deacon. The General Hospital was not a hospital in the modern sense, although it did have a sick ward and provided medical help for the poor. It served a wide range of social welfare functions, including an orphanage and an old age home. Bread was distributed at the Hospital to many poor who continued to live at home. The Hospital also provided lodging for poor transients. The deacons who directed the Hospital also arranged apprentice training for orphan boys and dowries for poor girls. Public begging was forbidden, but the deacons solicited help from the wealthy, much as the United Fund does today. The city government contributed generously, and specific public fines were earmarked for the Hospital, as were the royalties from the sale of certain religious books. The Hospital served transients and citizens, but Geneva was also crowded with religious refugees who needed help to get back on their feet. For these, other deacons administered the French Fund, to which Calvin contributed a large part of his salary.

During the last two decades of Calvin's life the four-fold ministry transformed Geneva and made it the Protestant city of God which became a model for Calvinists from Poland to New England. John Knox, who had observed the reformation in many cities, remarked, "In other places, I confess Christ to be truely preached; but manners and religion so sincerely reformed I have not yet seen in any other place."

5

Protesters on the Continent

Germany

Quite aside from the rise of Protestantism, the sixteenth century was a period of rapid change. Population rose rapidly. An increase in precious metals, first from mines in central Europe, then from the New World, combined with accelerating trade and rising population to spark a prolonged inflation. The price rise did not affect all classes and occupations equally; some profited and others suffered, but everywhere inflation introduced tensions into social, economic, and political relations. For two thousand years the Mediterranean had been the economic crossroads of the western world. Columbus and Vasco da Gama opened up new lands and new trade routes. Venice slowly slipped into golden decadence while Lisbon, Seville, Antwerp and Amsterdam built wharves and founded bourses to handle the merchandise of China and Peru. In France, England and Spain new monarchs tried to encourage and control commerce; gradually they built up bureaucracies which could make the royal will effective through the semi-feudal countryside.

The religious convictions of Erasmus, Luther, Calvin and Loyola owed little to these dynamic forces, but the impact of the reformers was heightened and shaped by them. Religious change never takes place in a vacuum. The reformation came to a Europe already undergoing profound transformation, and religion interacted with these forces and tensions.

The Holy Roman Empire of the German Nation was the most complex and populous state in Europe. The emperor, little more than a unifying figurehead, was usually from the Hapsburg dynasty, but seven leading princes (including three archbishops) had the right to elect the emperor. The Empire was a confederation held together by periodic diets whose various houses reflected the fragmentation of the Empire. Greatest in honor were the seven electors, but the most powerful were the several dozen major princes. Least important were the thousand and more free imperial knights, usually poor in everything but pride. Eighty-five free and imperial cities were registered at the Diet of Worms in 1521. A narrow patriciate of businessmen controlled the town councils almost everywhere. Most Germans were peasants and had no political voice either inside or outside the diets.

Luther's writings evoked support everywhere, but particularly in the cities, where humanism had prepared the ground among the patriciate. Even more enthusiastic were the lower classes, for Luther appealed to their intense religiosity, their anticlericalism, and their resentment against the flow of German money to Rome. His emphasis on the sacred nature of the lay vocation struck a responsive chord. Pro-Luther guilds often prodded reluctant town councils into authorizing Lutheran preaching, mainly by former priests, in the teeth of episcopal opposition. In several towns the Protestant reformation represented the final break with the bishop's authority as feudal overlord. In a few cases the bishops took the lead and converted their holdings into hereditary principalities. Usually the establishment of Protestantism entailed the closing of monasteries and convents and the confiscation of their income for educational and charitable purposes. Usually the town council acquired greater control over the local church, although city governments often exercised sweeping powers even before the reformation. It would be wrong to attribute the success of the reformation to economic and political considerations; religious considerations were usually primary. Economic considerations could sometimes help to keep a city in the Catholic camp, for the imperial government encouraged some cities to remain Catholic by lessening their tax assessment. Politically the safest course was to remain Catholic or at least Lutheran, yet many cities in southern Germany accepted a reformed faith that derived more directly from Zwingli or Martin Bucer than from Luther.

In the course of the sixteenth century roughly fifty Imperial cities decided for Protestantism, among them the great commercial centers of Augsburg, Nuremberg, Strasbourg, Hamburg and Lübeck. Mainz, Trier, and Cologne, the sees of the three Elector-Archbishops, remained Catholic but not without a struggle. In some cities both Catholic and Lutheran worship were tolerated, but in most instances the close union of church and state and the conviction that the church and the civic community should be co-extensive precluded toleration. The struggle for religious supremacy often resulted in exile for the losers; the sale of property, carts loaded with household goods, tearful departures from old neighbors, emigration and new beginnings were common experiences.

Far more important than the declining towns for the future of the Empire were the princes. Eventually most of the princes of central and northern Germany came to adopt Lutheranism. Several of Luther's friends on the faculty at Wittenberg were counsellors to the Elector of Saxony and helped gain his support. Philip of Hesse proved the most dynamic of the Lutheran princes and played a key role in German politics. Albert of Brandenburg, Grand Master of the Teutonic Knights, a Catholic crusading order which controlled vast stretches along the Baltic coast, secularized these lands, brought in Lutheran preachers, and proclaimed himself Duke of Prussia. Later the Elector of Brandenburg declared for Protestantism, as did the Dukes of Württemberg, Cleves, Saxony, and Mecklenburg.

Luther's attitude toward the princes was ambivalent. He

recognized the autonomy of the secular state and saw the authority of the princes as coming from God. Hence he gave obedience to the state a religious sanction. He was convinced that the medieval church had usurped jurisdiction in many areas, especially the control of marriage and morals; these he committed to supervision by the secular authorities. For Luther the secular and the religious spheres were distinct but not separate. The Christian congregation guided by the word of God had the right to decide doctrine, administer church property, and choose ministers. The congregational strain in Luther's ecclesiology had little immediate effect. In practice the Lutheran princes quickly took control of the churches in their territories, and Luther reluctantly accepted this as a temporary need during a period of re-organization, but their temporary control lasted as long as the princes, until 1918. Under their supervision visitation committees surveyed the needs of the local churches and made recommendations. Many princes issued a *Kirchenordnung* which regulated church affairs in their territory.

Inevitably the Lutheran princes and cities banded together to protect their interests. At the Diet of Speyer in 1529 the Catholic majority passed a decree which reasserted the ban outlawing Luther and forbade further religious change. This the Lutheran minority protested—the word *Protestant* was born. After an absence of nine years, Charles V returned to Germany to attend the Diet of Augsburg in 1530. On behalf of the Lutheran estates Philip Melanchthon drew up a confession of faith to present to the Emperor. In his *Augsburg Confession*, which remains a fundamental Lutheran doctrinal statement, Melanchthon tried to be as conciliatory toward the Catholics as possible, gliding over many difficulties. Luther would have preferred more candor, and four southern German cities had Capito and Bucer draw up an uncompromising statement of their faith. The Emperor and the Catholic estates rejected both confessions and threatened to use force. In consequence the Protestant princes and cities closed ranks and gathered at Schmalkalden to found the Schmalkaldic League to defend their faith.

In medieval theory Charles V was duty-bound to suppress Lutheranism. He would have done so gladly, for he saw in Luther a dangerous rebel. Why did he hesitate? Charles V was the most powerful emperor since Charlemagne, for he held the Hapsburg crown lands in southeast Germany and was king of Castile, Aragon, Naples, Sicily and hereditary prince of most of the Netherlands. His brother Ferdinand was king of Bohemia and of Hungary, and Cortes and Pizzaro conquered much of the New World for him.

Charles failed to act because his many lands multiplied his problems and his enemies faster than they increased his resources. Loyalty to his person was the only bond that held his empire together. His subjects in Europe alone spoke at least eight different languages. As king of Aragon, for instance, Charles had to deal with three different parliaments. Throughout his life he had two deadly rivals, Francis I of France and Sultan Suleiman the Magnificent. The Ottoman Turkish Empire was at its height, aggressive and confident, stretching from Algiers to Armenia, from Baghdad to Budapest. Charles had to fight the Turks in North Africa, before the gates of Vienna, and at sea in the Mediterranean. He also fought five major wars against France, which was sometimes in alliance with the Turks. Henry VIII was usually friendly but always untrustworthy, ready to ally with France for the smallest advantage. The pope and Venice distrusted Charles and resented his domination of Italy. Within Germany the princes had been virtually independent for centuries. Lutheranism gave many princes another way to prevent Charles V from building an effective imperial government that might threaten their independence. The Catholic princes, such as the Dukes of Bavaria, were as opposed to imperial domination as were the Protestants. The Emperor was chronically short of money. He needed the troops of the Lutheran princes and the money of the Lutheran towns if he was to defend the southeastern frontier of the Empire from the Turks. As long as France and the Turks threatened, the Schmalkaldic League had little to fear from Charles V.

The Truce of Nice in 1538 gave Charles a respite in Europe, although the Mediterranean war with the Turks continued. In Rome a circle of reformers led by Cardinal Gasparo Contarini were in the ascendent. Both Contarini and Charles sincerely felt that a theological compromise with the Lutherans was possible. After preliminary conferences at Hagenau and Worms, the Emperor arranged a theological summit conference at Regensburg in 1541. Melanchthon and Bucer served as the leading Protestant spokesmen, while Calvin attended as an advisor and Contarini guided the Catholic representatives. On questions such as the Trinity and Christology there was quick and cordial agreement. The high point of the conference was an agreement, engineered by Contarini, to a statement on justification which combined Lutheran and Catholic ideas in an uneasy compromise. Contarini was jubilant, but the conference soon broke down over the nature of Christ's presence in the eucharist. Neither side could honestly compromise. The conference never got into the thorny question of papal authority. Later a conclave of cardinals declined to accept the compromise on justification, although Contarini continued to defend it. Luther and Calvin denounced it, and Melanchthon came to believe that he had been misled into accepting it.

Regensburg marked the high tide of ecumenical attempts to hammer out a doctrinal compromise during the reformation era. In contrast to the bitter polemics common during the sixteenth century, Regensburg brought together in an atmosphere of mutual respect men who passionately wanted Christian unity. The Emperor too needed a solution that avoided religious war. But devoted as both sides were to conciliation, their commitment to revealed truth, as they saw it, overrode every other consideration.

The outbreak of the fourth Hapsburg-Valois War in 1542

postponed imperial action against the Lutherans, but the Peace of Crespy in 1544 again gave Charles a free hand, and he determined to use force. Pope Paul III pledged generous financial support and a papal army. Skillfully Charles played on the divisions and weaknesses among the Lutheran leaders; he detached Elector Joachim of Brandenburg and Duke Maurice of Saxony from the Schmalkaldic League by promises of preferential treatment. When Charles declared war in 1546, the League forces were superior but frittered away their early advantages as Charles gathered his troops. The next spring he defeated a Lutheran army at Mühlberg; the League collapsed after Charles had taken prisoner John Frederick of Saxony and Philip of Hesse.

It seemed that Charles could dictate a religious solution, but difficulties quickly arose. Friction developed between the Emperor and the Pope over the Council of Trent. The murder of the Pope's son by the Emperor's agents and his dominance of Italy made Paul III veer toward a French alliance. Meanwhile the Emperor rammed through the Diet at Augsburg a decree governing religion. It was entitled the *Interim* because it was to last until an ecumenical or a national church council settled the religious problem. The doctrine laid down in the *Interim* was fundamentally Roman Catholic, but allowed Protestants a few concessions such as clerical marriage and communion under both bread and wine. The Emperor's Lutheran allies received more generous treatment, but neither Lutherans nor Catholics were satisfied. Many Lutheran cities in northern Germany, led by Magdeburg, openly defied the *Interim*. It is problematic whether the Emperor's ersatz religion could have worked even if he had enough zealous Catholic priests to staff every Lutheran parish and enough Spanish troops to protect them. He had few of either. Often Lutheran pastors continued at their posts, making as few concessions to the imperial decree as possible. Such a situation could not continue long. Several Lutheran princes opened communications with Henry II, the new king of

France, who revived French claims to Flanders, Milan and Naples and hurled 35,000 troops toward the Rhine. In Germany a sudden rising of the Lutheran princes, this time united, sent Charles scurrying south of the Alps. The war dragged on until the peace of Augsburg, 1555, which brought Germany seventy years of peace. The treaty gave Lutherans legal standing and allowed local princes and cities to choose between the two faiths. Shortly afterwards Charles V gave up trying to cope with the problems of Europe and retired to a Spanish monastery. His brother Ferdinand took the imperial title and the traditional Hapsburg crown lands, while his son Philip II became King of Spain and acquired his holdings in Italy and the Netherlands.

Luther died in 1546 and did not live to see the dark days of the *Interim*. Ill health and disillusion with many of his followers made him cantankerous during his declining years, but his charismatic presence insured Lutheran unity. After his death German Protestants were rent by theological quarrels. Philip Melanchthon might have inherited Luther's prestige, but his vacillating acceptance of the *Interim* stood in sorry contrast to the courage of his Magdeburg rival Flacius Illyricus. Strict Lutherans found Melanchthon too Calvinist in his eucharistic doctrine and too Catholic in his theology of grace. Calvinist teaching flourished at the University of Heidelburg and enjoyed princely patronage in the Palatinate and later in Brandenburg-Prussia. In the face of the Calvinist threat, Lutheran theologians united to produce the *Formula of Concord* (1577), a balanced doctrinal statement that some eight thousand pastors and many towns and princes signed. For the next two centuries Lutheran theologians concentrated on defending its orthodoxy in massive treatises that recall the systematic methods of medieval scholasticism. In many parts of the Empire Lutheranism continued to grow and consolidate during the decades after 1555.

Lutheranism also triumphed in Scandinavia. Merchants and students returning from Germany first spread Lutheran ideas, but much more important was a complex web of political events. Since the Union of Kalmar of 1397 the Danish king ruled nominally over all Scandinavia; in practice local bishops and magnates and traditional customs and laws constricted his power. Christian II determined to convert this loose dynastic union into a centralized renaissance state. The pope backed his efforts, but in Sweden they soon provoked a national resistance movement led by Gustavus Vasa, who was elected king of Sweden in 1523. Gustavus confiscated most of the wealth of the church to meet his debts and encouraged Lutheran preachers. Later the king tightened his control over the church, which retained episcopacy. There was little doctrinal strife, and not until 1593 did the Swedish church officially adopt the *Augsburg Confession*, the mildest of Protestant creeds.

Christian II's attempt to establish an autocratic state also failed in Denmark. He succeeded in taking control of the Danish church, but his policies led to war with Sweden and Lübeck, and his efforts to undermine the nobles caused them to depose him in favor of his uncle Frederick. The new king favored Lutheranism, imported preachers from Germany, and entered the Schmalkaldic League. Subsequently Denmark encouraged Lutheranism in its dependencies, Norway and Iceland, as did Sweden in Finland.

France

The tragic story of the French reformation falls into four acts. From 1520 to 1550 there was a spontaneous growth as the ideas of Luther, Bucer, and Zwingli circulated among all levels of society. Converts among printers, merchants and the lower clergy were the most important. Persecution was bloody but sporadic. During these early years Protestantism was a movement rather than a church; there were few organized communities and fixed pastors; a group would meet secretly for prayer and Bible reading, and perhaps an itinerant minister might celebrate the Lord's supper. Most

Protestants tried to boycott the local Catholic parish except for baptisms and marriages.

The organizational phase ran from 1550 to 1562 as Calvin and Geneva made their influence felt. Calvin insisted that Protestants must systematically avoid Catholic services and organize their own church structures. Ministers were in short supply, and many nascent congregations applied to Geneva for help. Calvin sent all the men he could and certified others with letters of recommendation. By 1561 there were over two thousand Protestant congregations in France, and Calvinists began to worship openly, sometimes in confiscated Catholic churches. More often they gathered in barns or the homes of nobles or simply out of doors. At times their meetings became a show of strength; in August, 1560, seven thousand filled the marketplace at Rouen for a sermon, while five hundred armed Huguenots encircled the gathering to insure that the service remained undisturbed.

As far as conditions allowed, Huguenot communities modelled themselves on the church of Geneva, but France was a large country and needed a more elaborate structure. A consistory of a minister and lay elders governed the local church. Local churches sent delegates to the district assembly and these in turn reported to the provincial synod. The capstone was the periodic national synod. The first national synod met secretly at Paris in 1559 and drew up the Gallican Confession of Faith. Of course Calvin had no direct control over the French church, but the prestige of Calvin and Theodore Beza, his successor at Geneva, carried great weight on theological questions. Printing books for the French church became a major industry at Geneva.

During most of his reign Henry II (1547-1559) was preoccupied with war against Spain, but in his last months he unleashed a savage persecution to annihilate Protestantism. After his accidental death in a tournament France did not enjoy a strong king until 1594. His widow Catherine de Medici tried to shore up royal power for her sons, Francis II, Charles IX and Henry III, by steering a middle course between rival religious and noble factions. The development of the Calvinist church was engulfed by the ensuing power struggle. Especially from 1559 to 1562 an unusually large number of nobles flooded into the church and converted it into a political-military faction. Nearly half the French nobles became Protestant, whereas only ten percent of all Frenchmen were converted. Among the new recruits were the Bourbon Prince of Condé and the King of Navarre together with the three Coligny brothers, Admiral Gaspar, the General François, and Cardinal Odet, who insisted on retaining his title even after his conversion. Leadership on non-theological matters passed from Calvin and Beza to these princes who turned their vast holdings in southern France into bastions of Calvinism. The pyramidal structure of the Huguenot churches also organized French Calvinists for politics and war.

The nine civil wars that wracked France from 1562 to 1598 constitute the third phase of Huguenot history. Calvin counselled patience under persecution, but the Huguenot nobles were bred to a different psychology and had the power to resist. Reluctantly Calvin conceded that armed rebellion was permissible against a tyrannous, persecuting monarch provided that a Prince of the Blood assumed leadership. Condé filled that stipulation. At first the French Wars of Religion were fought to determine whether Protestantism would be tolerated, but increasingly they became battles between noble factions for control of the government. For mercenaries on all sides war became simply a way of life and an excuse for plunder. The Huguenots looked to England and the German princes for help; the Catholic League was aided by Philip II of Spain. Both sides destroyed churches and perpetrated massacres, but the Catholics, being stronger, carried through the greatest massacres, including the horror of St. Bartholomew's Day in 1572 when three thousand Huguenots perished in Paris alone. Many of the leaders on both sides fell to assassins.

The assassination of Henry III in 1589 left the Huguenot

Henry of Bourbon-Navarre as the heir apparent. French tradition and law required that the king be Catholic, and many members of the Catholic League preferred to see France under Spanish dominance than under a Calvinist king. Henry IV had always been an opportunist; in 1594 he switched religion for the fifth time and declared himself a Catholic, whereupon opposition melted. After concluding peace with Spain in 1598, he issued the Edict of Nantes which recognized Catholicism as the official religion of France but gave Calvinists full liberty of conscience, widespread freedom of worship, and many civil and political rights. Nowhere else in Europe save Poland was so great tolerance given a religious minority.

The Edict of Nantes opened the fourth phase of French Protestantism. The civil wars had sapped the religious dynamism of the Huguenots, who remained a tenth of the nation, mainly an elite of merchants, nobles and townsmen. Gradually Louis XIII and Louis XIV restricted their rights by a narrow interpretation of the Edict, meanwhile undermining their political power as a threat to the unity of the French state. After a campaign of petty persecutions Louis XIV revoked the Edict of Nantes and forced most Huguenots to emigrate or accept Catholicism.

The Low Countries

Germany, a mosaic of small principalities, allowed the local prince to determine the religion of his subjects. France, a unitary monarchy, solved the problem of religious diversity by forcing Henry IV to conform to the religion of the majority but allowing toleration for the Protestant minority. The rise of Protestantism took still a different course in the Netherlands: partition into Catholic Belgium and the Protestant Dutch Republic.

Charles V inherited the Netherlands from his Burgundian grandmother and was raised in the Flemish city of Ghent. Nowhere else in his multi-national empire were the cities so rich or the nobles so sophisticated and jealous of their local privileges. Charles wisely pampered them and used their resources to finance his far-flung enterprises, but his ruthless punishment of heretics in these personal domains contrasts with his practice in Germany. Here the Lutheran proto-martyrs went to the stake in 1523, as did the English Bible translator William Tyndale in 1536, but most of the victims were humble Anabaptists.

Philip II, the son and successor of Charles V, was never popular in the Netherlands. Raised in Spain, he never learned Flemish-Dutch which two-thirds of the Netherlanders spoke, although he could speak the French used by the Walloons in the southeast. After 1559 Philip never visited any of the seventeen Netherlands provinces but tried to rule them through regents stationed in Brussels. His policies were simple: increase taxes, strengthen royal control and stamp out heresy.

Philip's policies made revolutions inevitable. All his sub-jects resented him as a foreigner who taxed them for imperial concerns in which they had little interest. The nobles particu-larly saw his bureaucracy as a threat to their control of local offices and to traditional liberties. His Catholic subjects had no desire for an Inquisition on the Spanish model; Protes-tants saw their faith and their lives in deadly peril. From all directions the Netherlands were open to Protestant influ-ences. To the east were the German Lutheran states, and across the Channel lay Protestant England. Calvinism made early inroads in French-speaking Artois, Hainaut, and Namur.

In 1559 Philip issued orders establishing an Inquisition and reorganizing the church in the Netherlands. Influential nobles led by Count Egmont and William the Silent, the Prince of Orange, resigned from the government in protest, and many local officials simply ignored the orders from Madrid and Brussels; other nobles quietly discussed rebellion and drew up protests. Soon Calvinist mobs began smashing church windows and statues. Since local officials seemed paralyzed, in 1567 Philip sent the Duke of Alva at the head of ten thousand hardened troops into the Netherlands and imposed martial law. Alva's "Council of Blood" established a reign of terror. Counts Egmont and Hoorn, Catholics who tried to combine loyalty to the king with the protection of local traditions, were arrested, tried for treason, and executed as an example. Thousands died and tens of thousands fled. The military occupation proved expensive, so Alva decreed crippling taxes, particularly on trade. His brutality and taxes only intensified the opposition.

William of Orange worked in Germany to organize a motley army of refugees and mercenaries, but Alva's veterans smashed their invasion. In contrast, Calvinist rebels from Holland, Zeeland and Utrecht organized the famous sea beggars, who seized a series of coastal cities and defeated the Spanish fleet. Then they began to prey on Spanish shipping everywhere and to raid Spanish colonies. When Philip II became king of Portugal in 1580, they included the Portuguese colonies in their attacks and thereby laid the foundation of the Dutch overseas empire. Against the sea coast towns, which could be supplied by sea and were protected by a network of rivers, canals, islands and dikes, Alva's infantry proved ineffective.

In 1573 Philip replaced Alva with Don Luis de Requescens, who tried concessions and negotiations. William of Orange wanted a united Netherlands with religious toleration for all; each province would enjoy local autonomy, and William was even willing to allow Philip to reign provided he did not rule. But religious toleration was unacceptable both to Philip and to the extreme Dutch Calvinists who were the best fighters among the rebels. Wherever they gained power, Catholicism was outlawed.

On Requescens' death, Philip sent his half-brother Don Juan of Austria, hero of Lepanto and scourge of the Turks and Moriscos; but the Dutch situation needed more supple skills than knight-errantry. Indeed, Don Juan's diplomatic mission was compromised before it began by the "Spanish Fury" of 1576. The unpaid army mutinied and sacked Antwerp, leaving six thousand citizens dead. Despairing of negotiations, Don Juan could recommend nothing better than more soldiers and more fighting. Meanwhile Catholic Brussels welcomed William of Orange and joined the union to drive out the Spanish. His dream of a united tolerant Netherlands seemed within reach, but in the spring of 1578 a new wave of Calvinist iconoclasm broke out. Today this smashing of statues stands condemned because it destroyed so much art; Calvin, most of the leading ministers, and all the Calvinist political leaders condemned it for a more practical reason: nothing else alienated people so quickly from the Protestant cause. But the zealots would not be checked; they cited the commandment against graven images and saw themselves as Jehu (2 Kings 10) casting down the idols of Baal. When a Huguenot leader snatched up a gun to stop a follower atop a church, the man shouted down, "Sir, wait till I have smashed this idol and then I will die if you like." The desperate courage of the extreme Calvinists checked Spanish reconquest, but their intransigence also ruled out William's dream. As late as 1587 only about ten percent of the people of the Netherlands were Protestant, and without the Catholic majority the rebellion against Spain could never fully succeed.

In 1578 Don Juan died suddenly and Alessandro Farnese, the Duke of Parma, took command. If William of Orange is the Father of the Dutch Republic, Parma can claim to be the Father of Belgium. The finest general of the century, he combined high strategy with an uncanny feel for topography. By sharing danger and hardship with his men, he acquired a charismatic hold on Philip's polyglot army of Spaniards and Italians, Germans and Walloons. More important, he was a born diplomat, careful of the sensibilities of his allies, quick to exploit the weaknesses of his enemies. Within a year he cemented the Union of Arras which detached the southern Catholic provinces from William and the Dutch. Gradually his army cut off and captured one town after another.

William realized that his cause needed outside help; putting aside personal ambition, he sponsored foreign adventurers in search of a crown. First came the Austrian Archduke Matthias, then the French Duke of Anjou, and later the English Earl of Leicester. The last two had been suitors to Queen Elizabeth, and Leicester brought an English army to the Netherlands. The foreigners proved inept and alienated the Dutch. The Dutch fought well, but the Spanish army continued to advance.

Parma might well have captured Amsterdam as he did Ghent, Brussels and Antwerp had he not been blocked by the river-rent Dutch landscape which consistently favored the Dutch defense and by Philip II who ordered Parma's army to invade England in concert with the Spanish Armada of 1588. Parma had to suspend operations, although he saw clearly that the Armada had little chance of success. Two years later he had to rescue the Catholic cause in France by lifting a Protestant seige of Paris, allowing the Dutch breathing space to re-organize their army and launch a counter-offensive which went well until stymied by the river barriers.

The war dragged on until 1609, when Spain and the Dutch agreed to a twelve year truce. Later both sides were sucked into the Thirty Years War; Spain finally recognized the Dutch Republic's independence in the Treaty of Westphalia of 1648. The Dutch-Belgian border rests on the defensive barrier of the river system rather than on any historical, linguistic, or religious cleavage among the population. Half of Belgium is inhabited by Flemings who speak a Dutch dialect. Originally the Walloon cities had many Calvinists and Ghent and Antwerp were Calvinist centers. In contrast Groningen in the Dutch Republic was solidly Catholic during the war years and only gradually became Protestant in the seventeenth century.

During the seventeenth century Belgium remained part of the Spanish empire, which now allowed much local self government but not religious toleration. After the wars those Protestants who had not fled earlier were compelled to sell their property and emigrate. Belgium did not recover her previous prosperity, for the countryside was ravaged and the Dutch blocked the sea approaches to the great port of Antwerp. As the Catholic reformation took hold, Belgium enjoyed an interesting cultural life, which is best approached through the life and paintings of Peter Paul Rubens, but her cities seem rather provincial when compared to Amsterdam, which became the richest and most cosmopolitan city of the early seventeenth century.

The Dutch Republic practiced greater religious pluralism than any other European country of the seventeenth century. Even witch hunting, which elsewhere claimed far more victims than religious persecutions, was almost unknown in Holland. Calvinists dominated the government, the army, and the business world. They did not believe in religious toleration as a principle; indeed, no religious group of the reformation era advocated toleration once it came to power. But toleration was good for business, and Holland lived by trade. More important, the Calvinists remained a minority, however dominant. Amsterdam housed a bustling Jewish ghetto which produced the philosopher Spinoza. There was a sprinkling of Lutheran nobles and peasants in the eastern provinces, and Mennonite communities in town and country. Some intellectuals took up Unitarianism which Socinian refugees imported from Poland. Descartes found the atmosphere congenial and spent twenty productive years in Holland.

Catholics were more numerous than the Calvinists. Their worship was outlawed but authorities winked at clandestine churches in private homes. Catholics were excluded from most public offices, and the government sometimes tightened the screws, for instance, executing several obstreperous Jesuits at Maastricht in 1639.

Dutch Calvinism was not a monolith. Early in the seventeenth century Jacob Arminius, a professor at Leiden, decried the narrow predestination of Calvin and Beza. Strict Calvinists rallied to its defense, but gradually the controversy broadened out. The Arminians found support among the merchant princes, but the House of Orange backed strict Calvinism and a national synod, so that provincial jealousies and jockeying for power blurred the theological issues. After the Synod of Dort decided for strict predestination in 1619, two hundred Arminian ministers lost their pulpits, but passions soon subsided. Calvinism in the Netherlands never developed into puritanism, and its harsh side was always muted by the traditions of Erasmian humanism and local currents of mysticism and piety which reached back to the medieval *devotio moderna*.

The moderate Calvinism which set the official tone of Dutch culture embraced hard work as a God-given duty. The sober businessman, his black clothing ornamented only by a rich white ruff, became the social ideal to which even nobles were expected to conform. Cleanliness became a Dutch fetish when elsewhere men accepted dirt as a condition of life (Queen Elizabeth, for instance, bathed once a year). Dutch furniture, so often featured in Vermeer's paintings, was ostentatious mainly by its solidity. The upper classes banded together into clubs and militia units which afforded companionship and protection should the lower class *grauw* become unruly. Prosperity and organized charity eased social unrest, but a gallows stood at every gate of Amsterdam to back up the law and order of the rich burghers who controlled the government and the church.

The middle class developed a taste, almost a mania, for paintings which reflected their ordered, prosperous lives. Hals and Rembrandt enable us to join their banquets and militia gatherings. In Rembrandt Protestant religious art reached its pinnacle; his psychological studies of Bible stories and of wrinkled old men in prayer contrast with the swirling, triumphant paintings with which Rubens was filling the baroque churches of Catholic Flanders. Both deeply religious, Rubens in Antwerp and Rembrandt in Amsterdam worked less than a hundred miles apart, yet civilization separates their art, a civilization founded by John Calvin.

6

Reform in Britain

Henry VIII

In 1509 bluff Prince Henry succeeded Henry VII, the grim and parsimonious founder of the Tudor dynasty. The new reign augured well, for Henry had a strong will and a keen intelligence which humanist teachers had sharpened on theology, foreign languages and a wide range of classical authors. Young Henry seemed a masterful monarch; healthy and handsome, he cut a striking figure both at court and in tournaments and wrestling matches, a sport at which no Englishman was strong enough, or foolish enough, to best the King. His lavish court evoked admiration from tax payers rather than murmurs, for the splendor of the King was the glory of his people.

Cardinal Wolsey dominated the royal administration during the first twenty years of Henry's reign. As a butcher's son, Wolsey's best chance for advancement lay through the church, and he made the most of it. Not untypical, he was essentially a civil administrator who financed his career by a chain of benefices that included the bishoprics of Lincoln and Tournai and the archdiocese of York; Wolsey never visited York until the last months of his life. As chancellor Wolsey relieved Henry of paperwork, even summarizing major treaties lest the king become bored with reading them.

Henry wanted glory, and glory came from war. Wolsey

recognized that England could not compete with France and the Hapsburg monarchy as an equal, but England could take advantage of their rivalry by assuring victory to one side or the other. Since Henry and Wolsey tended to confuse intrigue with statesmanship, their diplomacy became devious and complex, but generally they favored the Hapsburgs against France, a choice conditioned by trade ties with Flanders and Henry's belief in the traditional English claims to the French crown. Henry fought three wars against France and one as her ally. Twice the wars against France also involved war against Scotland and brilliant English victories, but on the Continent English armies achieved little and ate up enormous sums. The expenses of his foreign adventures go far toward explaining Henry's reliance on Parliament and his exactions from the church.

On the eve of the reformation English Catholicism displayed the same abuses found on the Continent. The leading bishops were absentees appointed by the crown as a reward for their services to the government. The local clergy were usually poor, uneducated, and lethargic, often the butt of the parish jokes. Lutheran ideas circulated among the cultivated from 1520 onwards and won over small circles, notably the group that gathered at the White Horse Tavern in Cambridge and later produced half a dozen Protestant bishops and as many martyrs. Remnants of Lollard anti-clericalism, demand for a vernacular Bible, and rejection of transubstantiation prepared many in the lower classes for Luther's teachings. Yet the ultimate triumph of Protestantism in England, even more than on the Continent, depended on government co-operation; Tudor England underwent four major shifts of religion, and each depended on the ruler.

Although more superstitious than devout, Henry VIII seemed attached to Catholicism; he attended mass daily and even wrote (or had ghost written) a defense of the seven sacraments against Luther, who deemed it worthy of a long refutation. True enough, the King desired to control the church, but friction with the papacy was nothing new, and accommodations could have been worked out had not the dark eyes of Anne Boleyn captured Henry. Although not particularly lecherous for a renaissance king, Henry had enjoyed a number of mistresses and produced a bastard son. Anne Boleyn had seen her sister Mary used by Henry and then put aside; she determined that royal mistress was not enough, that she must be Henry's wife. The more she resisted Henry's advances, the more his passion grew.

Catherine of Aragon was vulnerable as queen. She had failed to produce a male heir, and Henry never forgave this failure; in part his masculine pride was involved, in part he wanted a son to insure an untroubled succession. Furthermore, Henry's marriage to Catherine had required a papal dispensation since she had once been the bride of Arthur, Henry's older brother who died in 1502. If the dispensation was invalid, then a divorce (more properly an annulment) was possible which would leave Henry free to marry Anne and beget heirs. Henry soon became convinced that the pope had exceeded his powers in granting the dispensation, for did not Leviticus 20:21 state: "If a man shall take his brother's wife, it is an impurity...they shall be childless." No pope could loose what scripture had bound. Henry conveniently brushed aside other passages (Deuteronomy 25:5; Matthew 22:24) which authorized marriages such as his with Catherine. When Wolsey suggested a far better line of canonical argument, which might have secured the divorce without asking the pope to declare that his predecessor had acted beyond papal powers (something popes are singularly reluctant to do), Henry indignantly insisted on his own approach.

Even more fatal for Henry than the weakness of his legal case, Clement VII dared not decide for him because Charles V dominated Italy and supported his aunt Catherine of Aragon in contesting the divorce. English popular opinion also strongly favored Catherine and loathed Anne Boleyn as a siren who had bewitched the King. In the circumstances

Clement decided to stall for time: Henry, Charles, Catherine or Anne might die; more likely, Clement hoped that Henry's passion for Anne might cool as it had for her sister and others. Clement's plausible strategy backfired totally. Henry determined to force a favorable decision by applying pressure to the English church by a series of laws that rejected papal authority and brought the English church under royal control.

Wolsey's failure to secure the divorce cost him the King's favor; he was stripped of his offices, and only a timely death in 1534 saved him from treason charges. Thomas Cromwell, Wolsey's talented agent, gradually gained royal favor and orchestrated the King's attack on the clergy. Cromwell sincerely believed in state control of the church; slowly the royal attack became less a tactic to win the divorce and more a matter of conviction and settled policy by the King. Henry and Cromwell used statutory law as the instrument of their policy; Parliament, long hostile to the pope, Wolsey and the clergy, needed little encouragement. The most important of the new laws was the Act of Supremacy of 1534 which declared Henry "only supreme Head of the Church and Clergy of England." Henry used his new position as supreme head to increase taxes on the church.

Since the crown still needed money, Henry and Cromwell determined to suppress the eight hundred and fifty English monasteries and convents for the benefit of the crown. Unlike Luther and Calvin, Henry launched no attack on the nature of monastic life; more pragmatic, the government argued that the monasteries had ceased to serve society effectively and monastic discipline had decayed beyond recall. The suppression took two stages: in 1536 all monasteries with an income of less than two hundred pounds per year were suppressed "forasmuch as manifest, vicious, carnal and abominable living is daily used and committed." The smaller houses were contrasted with the greater monasteries "wherein, thanks be to God, religion is right well kept and observed." Three years later the government suppressed the greater monasteries. Before suppression the government sent around visitors to inspect the houses and dig up scandals, but mainly to fill out a detailed record of their wealth, which came to some £165,000 a year, mostly in rents. Most of the monastic land was incorporated into the royal estates, part was sold, but very little was given away. Some of the income had to be earmarked for pensions to the former monks, friars and nuns. Several former abbots did handsomely, but the nuns particularly got a pittance which inflation steadily reduced. Henry, keen on chastity for others, did not have the former monks and nuns released from celibacy. Monasticism, after eight hundred years on the English religious scene, disappeared utterly until the nineteenth century when monasteries following the ancient rules were revived in both the Anglican and Roman communions.

The break from Rome aroused surprisingly little opposition within the English church; only one bishop, John Fisher of Rochester, and a handful of monks refused to take the oath recognizing the royal supremacy and were accordingly executed for treason. The most famous victim was the former chancellor and renowned humanist, Sir Thomas More. Serious opposition appeared only with the Pilgrimage of Grace of 1536, a series of four armed uprisings of which the most important was in the north under Robert Aske. In part, these were reactions to the economic hard times and the growth of royal power in semi-feudal Yorkshire and Lancashire; in part they were protests against the dissolution of the smaller monasteries and the Protestant tendencies of Henry's new favorites, Cromwell, Archbishop Thomas Cranmer, and Hugh Latimer. The Pilgrims quickly gathered a large army; Henry reacted by sending the royal army north under his best general, the Duke of Norfolk, but no battle was joined. Rather Norfolk promised a general amnesty to the rebels and a hearing for their grievances, whereupon the rebels dispersed. Later Norfolk rounded up the leaders, who were tried and executed for treason. The Pilgrimage provided the government with an additional pretext for confiscating the larger monasteries. Under the Tudors there were half a dozen such rebellions motivated by a mixture of politics and religion. None succeeded, usually because their leaders only protested against specific policies and the monarch's evil councillors but could not agree on an alternative government. If the government felt strong enough, battle decided the issue; otherwise the government could promise reforms and wait for the rebellion to collapse of its own weight, wreaking vengeance later.

During the years following Henry's break from Rome religious policy oscillated as advocates of Catholic teaching and ritual struggled for royal favor against Cromwell, Cranmer and the other supporters of Protestant teaching. Always Henry remained the arbiter, and his religious preferences were conservative. The Protestants achieved their highpoint with the Ten Articles of 1536 which approached Luther's teaching on many points. Cromwell and Cranmer sponsored the publication of the Tyndale-Coverdale translation of the Bible. Cromwell coupled his religious policy with a projected alliance with the German Lutheran princes to offset a possible crusade of Francis I and Charles V against England. Cromwell cemented the alliance by persuading his royal master to marry Anne of Cleves, but Henry found "his Flanders mare" repulsive and could not consummate the marriage; accordingly he pensioned her off. Cromwell did not escape so lightly. Embarrassed by the marriage and annoyed by Lutheran demands for more doctrinal concessions, Henry rounded on Cromwell and had him executed for treason and heresy in 1540.

Even before Cromwell's fall the King swung to the more conservative theology expressed in the Six Articles of 1539 which upheld transubstantiation, clerical celibacy, and the necessity of private confession to a priest. Soon Lutheran books together with the Tyndale-Coverdale Bible were being burnt. Henry's conservative advisors during his declining years, the Duke of Norfolk and Bishop Stephen Gardinier, supported the royal supremacy over the church no less than did Cromwell and Cranmer. Two days after Cromwell's execution Henry VIII had three Catholics hanged as traitors for rejecting royal supremacy and three Protestants burnt as heretics for doctrinal error. This studied impartiality gave clear warning to all.

Henry's last years were marked by obesity, bad health and more marital problems. Anne Boleyn's pregnancy, which hurried their wedding, disappointed Henry with a daughter, Elizabeth. The King quickly tired of Anne and gave a ready ear to the flimsy charges of adultery that Cromwell contrived. After Anne's beheading, Henry married Jane Seymour who died after the Caesarian delivery of a son. Henry hardly noticed her passing amidst the banquets for young Edward. After his divorce from Anne of Cleves, Henry fell into dalliance with Catherine Howard, the spirited niece of the Duke of Norfolk who encouraged their affair. Fittingly they married on the day Cromwell was beheaded. The bride thrilled the old King, but meanwhile an informer accused her to the royal council of a premarital affair with a young courtier. Even when confronted by the courtier's confession, Henry rejected the accusation at first, but evidence soon mounted that Catherine had enjoyed two lovers after her marriage with Henry. This was treason. Catherine and the young men were executed for befouling the royal bed, the King's own amours being quite irrelevant in an age which accepted the double standard. In 1543 Henry contracted his sixth and happiest marriage with Catherine Parr. Twice a widow herself, Catherine was more a nurse than a wife to Henry. She gathered his three children together for the first time into a household that brought comfort to the cantankerous old King. Catherine was a convinced Protestant and supervised the education of Elizabeth and Edward in her faith; Mary, Catherine of Aragon's daughter, was older and unbending in her Catholicism. All three children had quick minds, so Catherine put the two girls to translating the religious writings of Erasmus; Catherine herself wrote and published two books of piety.

Edward VI and Mary I

Toward the end of Henry's reign Norfolk and Gardiner fell into disgrace; indeed, Norfolk survived only because Henry died the day before his execution was scheduled. The two conservative leaders spent the next reign in the Tower of London. Edward VI was only eleven years old at his accession; actual rule fell to the royal council, whose dominant figure was the young King's uncle, who assumed the titles of Lord Protector and Duke of Somerset.

England faced several major problems. Somerset invaded Scotland in an effort to extend Protestantism and English rule, winning a brilliant victory at Pinkie in 1547; but occupying Scotland proved more difficult than defeating the Scottish army. Moreover, France honored her old alliance with the Scots so that the English government, on the verge of bankruptcy, had to buy peace by surrending Boulogne. Henry's last war with France had been so expensive that much of the royal estate, including the monastic lands, was sold off, thereby permanently reducing the royal income from rents. Both Henry and Somerset resorted to the debasement of the coinage, but this palliative merely fueled inflation. Economic and religious discontent sparked rebellions in western and eastern England; the government crushed them, but Somerset's arrogance and his weakness in the crisis alienated the council, which supported the Earl of Warwick (later Duke of Northumberland) in taking over power in 1547 and executing Somerset for treason.

Both Somerset and Northumberland were Protestant in sympathy, as was the young King and the leading members of the council. The council arranged for Parliament to repeal the Six Articles of Henrician Catholicism. Religious images were removed from the churches, both wafer and wine were given at communion services, and the clergy were allowed to marry. In 1549 an Act of Uniformity replaced the Latin mass with Archbishop Cranmer's First Prayer-book, largely based on a Lutheran liturgy by Martin Bucer, but this proved only a stopgap.

Because England had few major Protestant theologians, Cranmer secured professorships at Cambridge and Oxford for Martin Bucer, Peter Martyr Vermigli and other continental divines. Helped by their advice Cranmer began to revise English canon law and worship. His eucharistic ideas now reflected the teaching of Geneva and Zurich. Cranmer's Prayer-book of 1552 was far more radical than its predecessor; many ceremonials were dropped or simplified, and the Swiss idea of communion as a memorial service and spiritual gift received in the heart alone became paramount. Most of the passages in the Prayer-book derive from medieval missals or earlier Protestant liturgies, but Cranmer recast them into stately English cadences which have worn well over the centuries and still serve Anglican worship.

Edwardian Protestantism reached its high tide in the Forty-Two Articles of 1552, a detailed credal statement that contained nothing Calvin would reject, although he might have preferred greater precision on several points. The Articles condemn Catholics and Anabaptists outright, and Luther could never have subscribed to their eucharistic teaching. To help the people understand Protestant doctrine, the Articles command that the *Book of Homilies* be read at church services. Many of the homilies, which continued in use under Elizabeth and the early Stuarts, dealt with prayer, sobriety and other neutral subjects, but many attacked Roman teachings, and their constant repetition over several generations from thousands of pulpits helped make England a Protestant country.

Early in 1553 Northumberland saw that Edward VI was dying. If Mary became queen, she would certainly bring back

Catholicism and probably have Northumberland executed. Hence the Duke persuaded the dying king to will the crown to Lady Jane Grey, whom the Duke married to his son. To further insure his continued power, Northumberland kept Edward's death a secret until Lady Jane could be proclaimed queen simultaneously throughout England. His plan collapsed as soon as Mary raised her standard and entered London in triumph on August 3, 1553. Deserted by all Northumberland went to the Tower and the block. Henry VIII's fears over a female succession proved groundless. Such was the popularity and power of the Tudor dynasty that both his daughters succeeded easily, even though both had been officially declared bastards and both brought with them a change of religion for the nation.

Mary devoted her reign to a single goal—the re-establishment of Catholicism in Enland. She never stopped to weigh the political wisdom of her goal; lacking the shrewdness of the other Tudors, she saw politics as a simple application of religious and moral principles. Her simplicity and stubbornness made an otherwise kindly woman into a symbol of cruelty as Bloody Mary.

At the outset she was lenient, personally intervening to save Lady Jane from execution. The foreign professors were helped to leave the country. Eight hundred English exiles joined them, a Protestant elite who studied theology, worship, and church organization in Frankfurt, Zurich, Strasbourg and Geneva to prepare for the day when they could return to England. Mary had holders of monastic lands confirmed in their possessions but ousted twelve Edwardian bishops and replaced them with Catholics; she convened Parliament to repeal the Edwardian religious legislation and restore Catholic worship.

Mary was thirty-seven at her accession; her Catholic restoration would be temporary unless she could beget an heir. Half Spanish herself, she inclined to Philip of Spain. Still young and handsome, Philip could also provide the power to insure the triumph of Catholicism in England. Parliament pleaded with Mary to marry an Englishman, otherwise England might become just another province in the empire the Hapsburgs had assembled by clever marriages. Even though the marriage contract carefully excluded Philip and the Spaniards from any power in England, xenophobic Englishmen linked Mary and her faith with foreign power; a nationalist, Protestant rebellion broke out in Kent which was stopped only at the bridges of London. The rebel leaders together with Lady Jane Grey were executed; Elizabeth may have been implicated but was released for lack of evidence. Nothing daunted, Mary went ahead with the disastrous marriage. Philip was an unloving husband who spent much of his time abroad, and Mary failed to conceive the child on whom Catholic hopes rested.

Mary was personally responsible for launching a concerted religious persecution which claimed three hundred victims from 1555 to 1558. Aside from Cranmer, four other bishops and nine gentlemen, the victims were almost all ordinary people: weavers, tailors and butchers. These were hardly a threat to the regime and the executions, far from serving as a warning, only disgusted the nation. John Foxe's *Book of Martyrs*, which describes the executions in vivid detail, became favorite reading for centuries of Protestants and identified popery with repression for the English-speaking world.

Sterility was the characteristic of Mary's reign. Neglected by her husband, she finally realized that she would never have a child, that her policies had alienated her people from her faith, and that her work would die with her. The Spanish alliance dragged England into a war with France and led to the loss of Calais, the last English toehold on the Continent. The loss was a blessing since it allowed England to take full advantage of its insular position in war and diplomacy, but Mary felt the loss so bitterly that she claimed at her death that doctors would find *Calais* engraved on her heart. Her religious policy rested on restoration and repression; attempting to turn back the clock to the early years of her father, she never discovered the vibrant forces of the new Catholicism that were reforming Italy and Spain. Her government relied on legislation and pompous processions but made little effort to make the common people understand Catholic teaching; characteristically it failed even to reply to Loyola's ardent offer to train English priests. When Mary died November 17, 1558, most Englishmen were not yet convinced Protestants, but they rejoiced at her passing and Londoners spent the night dancing and lighting bonfires to welcome Queen Elizabeth and a new era.

Elizabeth I

Like her half sister, Elizabeth had endured a difficult childhood, alternately pampered and thrust aside by her father, and imprisoned by Mary; but unlike Mary she emerged poised and versatile, knowing her goals but testing every wind of fortune before plotting her course. The Spanish ambassador Feria noted of the new Queen, "She seems to me incomparably more feared than her sister and gives her orders and has her way absolutely, as did her father."

The young Queen's most difficult problem was religion. Elizabeth never seriously considered continuing the Catholic restoration, for Mary's policies had weakened the Catholic cause, and many Catholics saw Elizabeth as Anne Boleyn's bastard with a tainted claim to the throne. But what sort of Protestantism would Elizabeth adopt, or be able to persuade the nation to accept? Elizabeth was not a zealot like Edward and Mary, but her Protestant convictions were genuine; she would have to consider political realities, but she was not a Machiavellian for whom religion was merely social cement. To Feria she praised the Lutheran Augsburg Confession; certainly she preferred a conservative Protestantism, with considerable ceremonial, vestments, episcopacy and even a celibate clergy. But her power to determine a religious settlement was never as great as Henry's. From the outset Elizabeth and her advisors realized that the Marian bishops would not co-operate and would have to be replaced by Protestants. There was only one source of new Protestant leaders: the elite who had gone into exile under Mary contained dozens of talented men eager to built a Protestant England, but they leaned to Zurich and Geneva, not to Wittenberg. The minimum acceptable to the Marian exiles was Cranmer's 1552 Prayer-book. The need for a compromise became apparent when a Protestant nucleus in the Parliament of 1559 redrafted the government's bill on religion along lines more radical than the Queen desired. The Elizabethan Settlement that emerged from their maneuvering was not a middle way between Rome and Geneva, as is often imagined, but a compromise between Elizabeth and the Marian exiles. The Thirty-Nine Articles adopted in 1562 sum up the basic teaching of the Anglican church. With minor revisions they repeat the Edwardian Forty-Two Articles in teaching a traditional view of the Trinity and of Christ, justification by faith alone, and predestination. Baptism, which is rightly administered to infants, and the Lord's Supper, in which Christ is present only spiritually, are the only sacraments. The Articles authorize an episcopal church polity under royal supervision. Several articles attack both Roman Catholic and Anabaptist teachings.

Most of the Marian exiles and their supporters had reason to be satisfied with this doctrinal statement, but the liturgy and church structures fell short of their goals. A few zealots such as Miles Coverdale and Thomas Sampson refused to serve as bishops under the Settlement, but most Anglican leaders saw it as a temporary expedient that they could live with until they gradually removed the vestiges of Romanism. Nearly the whole of Elizabeth's reign was a running fight between the Queen and the puritans who wished to purify the Church.

To these ardent Protestants many of the old feast days,

bowing to the altar, kneeling at communion, the use of the surplice at ordinary services and the cope for communion seemed silly and superstitious. Elizabeth quietly dropped Cranmer's revision of canon law and did nothing about the construction of efficient machinery, such as Geneva possessed, for discipline and the improvement of morals. She recognized that in most of England's seven thousand parishes the old Marian clergy would have to continue, since there were too few trained ministers to replace them. She had a healthy distrust both of their preaching skills and their devotion to Protestantism; consequently she ordered the reading of the *Book of Homilies*, which she valued highly and revised with her own hand. To zealous Protestants, a non-preaching minister was a contradiction in terms.

At first the puritans tried to work through Convocation, the assembly of bishops and leading churchmen, but in 1563 their proposed reforms fell one vote short. They then shifted their attack to Parliament. Elizabeth distrusted the puritans in Parliament, which she convened only ten times for a total of 140 weeks in her reign of forty-five years. When the puritans in the Parliament of 1572 introduced a bill to allow ministers to drop ceremonies they found objectionable, the Queen forbade the introduction of bills on religion without her specific approval and ordered the bishops to enforce the obnoxious ceremonies. When several puritans later tried to introduce a bill to replace the Book of Common Prayer with a Genevan Book of Discipline, Elizabeth stopped debate and jailed the proponents.

This petty persecution led Thomas Cartwright and many puritans to reconsider the whole structure of church government and relation of church and state. Cartwright argued that bishops should be abolished and each congregation should elect its own minister; each local church should be governed by a presbytery of the minister and lay elders. The government had Cartwright removed from his Cambridge professorship, whereupon he retired to Geneva and continued to write. Even more extreme was Robert Browne, whose *Treatise of Reformation without Tarrying for Any* mocked Anglican worship for "babbling prayers, popish attire, and foolish disguising" and advocated separation from the established church. Unimportant under Elizabeth, English separatism later grew to a powerful movement which foreshadowed many developments in American Protestantism.

Other puritans tried to build their own church inside the Anglican establishment by endowing lectureships for puritan preachers within many rich parishes. Others set up the *classis* movement, virtually a Presbyterian national church structure which simply ignored the official hierarchy. The high tide of Elizabethan Puritanism passed shortly after the defeat of the Spanish Armada in 1588. It was more difficult for puritans to pose as super-patriots after the passing of the Catholic threat. The deaths of Leicester, Walter Mildmay, and Francis Walsingham deprived the puritans of influential sympathizers within the government. Furthermore the puritan Marprelate tracts, which were printed on secret presses, backfired because of the bitterness of their attacks on the bishops ("poisoned, persecuting priests, petty popes, proud prelates, enemies of the Gospel") and the clergy ("dumb dogs, lewd livers, so many ignorant and atheistical dolts").

The chief reason for the decline of Elizabethan puritanism was the growing strength of moderate Anglicanism. In England as everywhere else, education for the clergy was improving; better clergymen were preaching better sermons. A new generation of ministers and bishops arose for whom Anglicanism was not a temporary compromise but a rich tradition. Bishops such as Lancelot Andrews, Richard Bancroft, and William Laud combined eloquence, support for episcopal government under state supervision, and an appreciation for the beauty of Anglican worship. The classic defense against puritanism was *The Laws of Ecclesiastical Polity*, which Richard Hooker wrote against Cartwright in the last decade of the century. On most points of theology Hooker approaches Calvin, but his serene quality of mind recalls Aquinas. For philosophic breadth, depth of learning, and majesty of expression (although too Ciceronian for today's taste) no previous book in English bears comparison with Hooker's masterpiece.

Elizabeth's government did not practice toleration since it was convinced that stability rested on religious uniformity; William Cecil, the Queen's chief minister, explained, "The State could never be in safety where there was toleration of two religions." The government wisely decided that slow suffocation was the best way to deal with Catholicism. Just as most priests accepted the new regime, so most Catholic laity felt that they could attend the Anglican service without detriment to their conscience as long as they avoided taking communion. Gradually and imperceptibly most became Anglicans in their hearts, just as the government had hoped.

This calm was broken by the flight of Mary Stuart, the Catholic Queen of Scotland, to England in 1568. Elizabeth could hardly send her cousin and fellow monarch back to execution in Scotland, but to allow Mary to leave England might involve another attempt to take Scotland with French or Spanish help, or even an invasion of England since Mary had a strong hereditary claim to the English throne. Elizabeth followed the safe course and imprisoned Mary. Even in prison Mary became the focal point of intrigues against Elizabeth. The first plot resulted in the Northern Rebellion of 1569, which was partly a Catholic revolt, partly a rising of the feudal northern earls against the central government and its parvenu ministers. When Elizabeth stood firm, the rebel army melted away and the earls fled abroad; the government later hanged one traitor from each rebellious village, some eight hundred in all.

The next year Pius V excommunicated Elizabeth and thereby encouraged Catholics to dethrone her at the first good opportunity. Catholics bitterly resented this papal decree because it faced them with conflicting loyalties to their faith and their Queen. Even in the Spanish Armada crisis most of them pledged their loyalty to Elizabeth. A militant new generation of priests trained at Douai and other special seminaries began to slip into England to minister to clandestine congregations, usually gathered in the homes of the nobles and gentry of northern England. They warned Catholics against attending Anglican services. Most avoided politics altogether, but a few such as Robert Persons decided, as had Theodore Beza, John Knox and Christopher Goodman earlier, that the religious persecutor was a tyrant who could be rightly overthrown.

Since the English government came to see Catholics as potential traitors, increasingly severe penal laws were passed against them. The shilling fine for failure to attend Anglican services was raised to a ruinous twenty pounds a month, more than most Englishmen made in a year. Catholics who went abroad without authorization forfeited their property; later Catholics who travelled more than five miles from their homes without a license incurred the same penalty. Attending mass could bring a heavy fine and a year's imprisonment; harboring a priest was a capital offense. Priests could be executed for entering the country or for converting anyone to Catholicism. Calling the Queen a heretic was treason. Some two hundred and fifty Catholics, mostly priests, were executed under Elizabeth. Under the Stuarts spasms of anti-popery agitation brought even more severe legislation. Had the laws been strictly enforced, Catholicism would have been wiped out; even sporadic enforcement largely achieved its goal since Catholics constituted only one percent of the English population when the repeal of the penal laws began in 1778.

The Elizabethan Settlement in religion also applied to Ireland, but the Anglican church came as a foreign intruder in Ireland where Catholicism was indentified with national resistance to expanding English power. Churches and ecclesiastical lands became Anglican property, but the government realized that a rigorous enforcement of the penal laws would drive Catholics to revolt. Even so, religion was a factor in the rebellions of 1569, 1579, 1596, 1641 and 1689. English rule never came close to stamping out Irish Catholicism, but for three centuries the English government forged a complex of laws to keep Catholics in political and economic subjection.

Since the foundation of the Tudor dynasty England's natural ally had been Spain. At first Philip II and Elizabeth fostered this friendship; Philip, at war with France, did not want to see Mary Stuart as queen of England since she was French by sympathy, upbringing and marriage. Elizabeth in turn cultivated Philip's friendship to protect English trade with the Netherlands, but hostilities were inevitable between the leading Catholic and Protestant powers. English privateers preyed on Spain's colonies and trade. In 1585 Leicester led an expeditionary force to the Netherlands to oppose Parma and the Spanish army, but Philip hesitated to invade England, for a Spanish invasion might serve to enthrone Mary Stuart and bring England under French influence. In 1586 Francis Walsingham, England's master counterspy, implicated Mary in still another plot against Elizabeth's life. Reluctantly Elizabeth signed the warrant for Mary's execution. Mary's death simplified the English question, for now Philip could assert a Spanish claim to England, which ran back through John of Gaunt to Edward III.

Attacking England presented formidable problems. Parma's army was the finest in Europe, but it lacked ships and suitable ports. The Spanish fleet was a motley collection of galleons and merchantmen, plus oar-driven galleasses and galleys better suited to the sunny Mediterranean than the wild winds of the Atlantic. Aboard would sail dauntless hidalgos, but the sailors included half-hearted Portuguese and impressed Italians. When the Armada sailed in May, 1588, the strategy was simple: proceed in a tight crescent formation to the Belgian coast, embark Parma's army and disgorge it on the English coast, defeating the English fleet should it interfere. Tactically the plan had little hope of success, as the best Spanish captains recognized. Even had Parma possessed a suitable port and sufficient lighters, the rondevous would have been delicate. Not only did the English fleet have better ships, better guns, better sailors and captains of the stature of Drake, Hawkins, Frobisher and Howard, it also enjoyed every advantage of geography since it would be fighting from its home ports. Perhaps Philip II imagined that the English would oblige and lash their swift ships to his hulks for a wild melee like Don Juan's triumph over the Turks at Lepanto; more likely the usually prudent King felt that God owed him a miracle. No Spanish miracle came, and his battle-shattered fleet had to limp home around the rocks of Scotland and Ireland amidst a wild gale. Rather the English claimed a Protestant miracle in the laconic statement on their commemorative coin: "God blew and they were scattered." The war dragged on for sixteen more years, as each side launched new invasion armadas which only demonstrated that the military technology of the age was incapable of amphibious operations with strategic results. In 1604 the peace-loving and impecunious James I signed a compromise peace.

Scotland

Even in Scotland, a poor country on the periphery of Europe, scattered converts were spreading Luther's ideas by the mid-1520s. The most noteworthy Protestant convert was John Knox (1505-1572), a former priest and thunderous preacher. Protestantism complicated the old division of Scots into pro-French and pro-English factions; generally the Protestants looked to the English for support and the Catholics to France. When Henry VIII's arrogance and plundering armies swung Scotch sympathy to France in 1547, the young Mary Stuart, Queen of Scots, was betrothed to the Dauphin, and

John Knox was chained to the oar of a French galley. Later freed by English intercession, Knox preached in England under Edward and ministered to English exiles at Frankfurt and Geneva under Bloody Mary. Meanwhile the French regent and soldiers in Scotland so alienated the nobles that in 1557 they proclaimed a covenant to preach Protestantism, adopted the English Prayer-Book, and began taking over Catholic churches. Knox returned and drew up the Scottish confession of faith. When the regent tried to stop them, the Calvinist nobles revolted openly and appealed for help to Queen Elizabeth, whereupon the English fleet sealed off Scotland from French reinforcements and the English army joined the rebels in forcing the French regent to sign the Treaty of Edinburgh of 1560 which required both French and English troops to withdraw from Scotland, thereby giving the nobles a free hand to abolish the mass and legalize Knox's confession.

The tragedy of Mary, Queen of Scots, serves as epilogue to the decisive phase of the Scottish reformation which climaxed in the Calvinist triumph of 1560. After Francis II of France died in 1560, his young widow Mary returned to Scotland to face Knox and the entrenched Calvinist Lords of the Congregation. Although allowed to remain a Catholic, she had to recognize Calvinism as the established religion. Lonely and emotional, Mary lacked the cool shrewdness of her cousin Elizabeth. She plunged into marriage with her cousin Lord Darnley, but soon came to despise his haughty stupidity and turned for affection and advice to her secretary David Rizzio. Outraged, Darnley and the Lords dragged him from her presence and stabbed him to death. Even the birth of a son (later James VI of Scotland and James I of England) did not heal the breach between Mary and her husband. Rather, she now turned to the Earl of Bothwell, who seems to have arranged the murder of Darnley under mysterious circumstances. Bothwell then divorced his wife, abducted the compliant Queen, and married her in a Protestant ceremony.

This last escapade so enraged opinion that Mary had to abdicate; after an attempt to seize power again, she fled to England where nineteen years of confinement and finally the headsman awaited her. Kingship was a deadly game for those who played with the heart and not the head.

After Mary's flight, the Earl of Moray served as regent for the infant King James and worked with Knox to consolidate the Scottish reformation. When Knox died in 1572, Andrew Melville took over leadership; less charismatic than Knox, he was a better scholar and even more insistent on fighting for a presbyterian church free from state control and for effective discipline on the Geneva model. As James grew up, he became convinced that royal power depended on control of the church, but control of the church could never be effective if ministers were elected by the people, as Melville demanded. Accordingly James tried to revive the dormant office of bishop and impose it on the Scottish church. Melville was not cowed by the King—at one meeting he snatched the King's sleeve and warned him that he was "God's silly vassal" and that "King James is subject to King Jesus." After James became king of England, he imprisoned Melville for four years in the Tower of London, then exiled him to France.

The struggle for control of the Scottish church continued under Charles I. At the first service at St. Giles Cathedral in Edinburgh under the Anglican ritual which Charles ordered in 1637, a woman threw her stool at the preacher and a riot broke out. Thousands of Scots signed a National Covenant to protect their worship and raised a national army. This revolt forced Charles to call the Long Parliament of 1642 and led to the English civil war and the subsequent execution of Charles.

In no other country was the impact of Calvinism so great as in Scotland, where it molded an austere and self-reliant people. Scotch Presbyterianism also developed an appreciation for learning which led to a re-organization of education from grammar schools to the universities and the highest literacy rate in Europe.

The Mood of the Times

The literary flowering of the renaissance came late to England and coincided with the reformation crisis. The greatest English writer of the early English renaissance was Sir Thomas More (1477-1535), the friend of Erasmus, whose witty translation of the Greek satirist Lucian betrays no hint that beneath his fur-trimmed lawyer's robes lay a hairshirt. More's greatest work, his Latin *Utopia*, opens with a critique of politics and society, then moves on to describe the island of Utopia ("Nowhere") which had developed a stable and just society through the use of pure reason. More does not propose Utopian institutions as a blueprint; rather these are constructs designed to highlight the absurdity and injustice of contemporary Europe. The absence of revealed religion in Utopia, far from representing an ideal, sharpens More's critique by contrasting the success of the Utopians who have only reason to guide them with the failure of Christians to apply their God-given faith to personal and social problems.

The humanist period of More's life ended when Henry VIII called him to royal service in 1518. Building on considerable political skill, hard work, and a reputation for honesty, More rose to be Lord Chancellor after Wolsey's fall in 1529. Despite the demands of his office, between 1529 and 1534 More wrote several bitter pamphlets against William Tyndale and other Protestant apologists. These niggling polemics and More's role of judge in heresy trials show his least attractive side. When More saw that Henry was bent on breaking with Rome, he resigned his offices and retired to prayer and writing. More's reputation as England's leading intellectual made his silence on the Oath of Royal Supremacy over the church more dangerous to Henry than the open opposition of lesser men. When efforts to entrap him failed, More was condemned on perjured evidence. The real measure of the man shines forth in his prison writings, especially the *Dialogue of Comfort against Tribulation* in which More meditates on Christ's passion to steel himself for death. Despite its serious subject the book abounds in kindliness, self-mockery, and in stories at once droll and devout. More won his struggle between human weakness and impending martyrdom, for even at the foot of the scaffold he managed a few sallies of wry humor.

William Tyndale (1492?-1536) was the Protestant counterpart of More. As a young priest he translated Erasmus' *Handbook of the Christian Soldier*, but later he became a disciple of Luther, whom he visited in Wittenberg. Skilled in Greek and Hebrew, he devoted his life to translating the Bible into English. Prior to the reformation Bible translations had been printed in all the major western European languages except English, largely because the English bishops associated vernacular Bibles with Wycliffe and the Lollards. Their opposition also forced Tyndale to work in Germany and smuggle his books into his homeland. His translation was clear, vigorous and rhythmical, at times even lyrical, and his turn of phrase underlies all early English translations, including the King James version. His New Testament appeared at Worms in 1526 and he translated six books of the Old Testament before he became caught up in a pamphlet war with More and other Catholic writers.

Tyndale's controversial works reveal a man indignant over religious abuses and ardent for social justice; no less than More, he condemns enclosures, which were driving farmers from the land to make room for sheep. Henry VIII enjoyed his *The Obedience of a Christian Man* (1528) because it flayed popes and bishops and exalted kingly power, but Tyndale lost favor when *The Practyse of Prelates* (1536) opposed the royal divorce. On the eucharist Tyndale followed Zwingli, but most his ideas came from Luther, for example: "faith only before all works and without all merits, by Christ's only, justifieth and setteth us at peace with God."

Tyndale spent his last years in the English enclave at Antwerp but was betrayed to the authorities of Charles V and executed a year after More's death.

Elizabethan Protestantism found its poetic voice in Sir Philip Sidney and Edmund Spenser. Sidney (1554-1586), the golden lad whose life expressed the ideals of his age, moved in the highest circles as Leicester's nephew and a royal favorite. In his early twenties he served as ambassador to the Emperor and to William of Orange. Intimate with Protestant leaders abroad, Sidney urged Elizabeth to launch a crusade against Spain and Catholic power. He visited the intellectual centers of Italy while abroad and even made a field trip into Hungary with a leading botanist. Well read in six languages, he discussed philosophy with the eccentric Italian Giordano Bruno and the Paris logician Peter Ramus and translated French Calvinist theology into English. He also translated the Psalms into verse, a favorite task among Calvinist poets. Against a puritan attack on poetry and drama Sidney wrote *The Apologie for Poetrie*, which ranks with the best literary criticism of the age.

Sidney's lasting monument is *Astrophel and Stella*, a sonnet sequence which soars above all previous English lyric poetry. The sequence ruminates on Sidney's love for Penelope Devereux, but sometimes his poetry deals with Christian themes:

> *Leave me ô Love, which reachest but to dust,*
> *And thou my mind aspire to higher things:*
> *Grow rich in that which never taketh rust:*
> *What ever fades, but fading pleasure brings.*
>
> *Draw in thy beames, and humble all thy might,*
> *To that sweet yoke, where lasting freedomes be:*
> *Which breakes the clowdes and opens forth the light,*
> *That doth both shine and give us sight to see.*
>
> *O take fast hold, let that light be thy guide,*
> *In this small course which birth drawes out to death,*

And thinke how evill becommeth him to slide,
Who seeketh heav'n, and come to heav'nly breath.
Then farewell world, thy uttermost I see,
Eternal Love maintaine thy life in me.

Sidney's death at thirty-one had the same romantic verve as his life. He joined Leicester's expedition to the Netherlands, where he constantly showed concern for the common soldiers. He was mortally wounded after he threw aside his armor that he might have no better protection than a friend; his last noteworthy act was a knightly gesture, giving his water canteen to a dying soldier whose "need was greater."

The life of Edmund Spenser (1552?-1599) as a minor cog in Elizabeth's Irish bureaucracy contrasts with the meteoric career of his friend Sidney; less noble as a man, Spenser was greater as a poet. He completed six books of the twelve he planned for his masterpiece, the *Faerie Queene*, a sprawling chivalric romance. In it Spenser fully indulges the renaissance taste for allegory. Spenser explains to Sir Walter Raleigh in the preface that his ethical-religious purpose "is to fashion a gentleman or noble person in vertuous and gentle discipline." Each book tells the adventures of a knight who stands for a key virtue; thus the Red Cross Knight of the first book is a model of holiness. Spenser leans on the ethical writings of Aristotle and Plato, but his allegory has a contemporary dimension. Glorianna the Faerie Queene is Elizabeth, to whom Spenser dedicated his poem. Duessa is at once falsehood and Mary Queen of Scots. Philip II, Leicester, Henry IV and many lesser figures have roles, but Spenser is too fine a poet to let his characters become bloodless abstractions or let history swallow up his story. Rich in sound effects and sensuous pictures, Spenser rarely disappoints the serious reader.

The greatest triumph of Elizabethan literature was drama, but the theater reflected little of the religious tensions of the era because few of the dramatists were deeply religious and because the rakes and rowdies who filled the pits wanted entertainment and not sermons.

The writer who best mirrors the religious crosscurrents of the generation following Sidney and Spenser is John Donne (1573-1631). Raised a Catholic, he took Anglican orders after his hopes of secular preferment faded. As Dean of St. Paul's Cathedral in London, he became the most fashionable preacher of the age, but his sermons are not easy; often sombre meditations on death freighted with learning and obscurity, they still flash with brilliant metaphors and memorable passages.

Donne wrote many of his best poems before twenty-five. For allegory, mythology and the sugared, musical verse of his age he had only contempt. His poems tried to capture the rhythms and vocabulary of ordinary speech, but his horror of commonplace expression led him to seek eccentric images to celebrate his passions. The flea whose bite mingles his blood with the blood of his mistress becomes inviolate and sacramental:

Oh stay, three lives in one flea spare,
where we almost, yea more than married are.
This flea is you and I and this
Our marriage bed, and marriage temple is.

For all his inventiveness Donne was typical of his age in hating nothing in politics and religion so much as novelty; his theological writings lump puritan and Jesuit together and condemn them for the same fundamental sin, innovation. Donne's *Ignatius His Conclave* is at once an essay in and parody of controversial theology; it pictures Loyola's descent into hell, where Satan gladly grants him second place lest he take over the whole infernal kingdom. For all that, recent scholars have argued that Donne's religious poetry, which he wrote at the end of his life, depends both in its structure and use of poetic imagination on Loyola's techniques for mental prayer. No Englishman better reflected the paradox and anguish of divided Christendom better than Donne:

Batter my heart, three-personed God; for You
As yet but knock, breathe, shine, and seek to mend;
That I may rise and stand, o'erthrow me, and bend

Your force, to break, blow, burn, and make me new.
I, like an usurped town, to another due,
Labor to admit You, but Oh, to no end!
Reason, Your viceroy in me, me should defend,
But is captived, and proves weak or untrue.
Yet dearly I love You, and would be loved fain,
But am betrothed unto Your enemy:
Divorce me, untie or break that knot again,
Take me to You, imprison me, for I,
Except You enthrall me, never shall be free,
Nor ever chaste, except You ravish me.

7

The Catholic Reformation

The Reformers of Italy

The last three chapters have traced the rise of Protestant churches in northern Europe. What of southern and eastern Europe? Why was the spread of Protestantism checked and rolled back in several places late in the sixteenth century? The fundamental answer to these questions is the Catholic or counter reformation. The attitude of rulers such as Philip II kept many areas Catholic. The Catholic church found increasingly effective ways to stifle the spread of Protestant ideas. Yet in the last analysis religion is a matter of head and heart. Had the Catholic reformation been only a hasty defense thrown up by rulers and churchmen to protect their vested interests, it could not have withstood the mighty blows of Luther and Calvin.

The roots of the Catholic reformation reach back to the late middle ages. At the end of the fifteenth century no serious observer questioned the need for church reform. At issue was the proper direction of reform. Who should take the lead? What should be saved and what discarded from medieval faith and practice? To these problems there was no single solution. During the opening decades of the new century in northern Europe Erasmus gave one answer, Luther another. In Italy men no less earnest were grappling with the same problem.

On the eve of the Reformation Julius II and Leo X presided over an ecumenical council, Lateran V, which met sporadically from 1512 to 1517. For the popes that Council was largely a counterstroke to the French invasions of Italy, but its official purpose was church reform. Its decrees condemned most of the abuses of the age, but the popes and bishops lacked the courage for genuine reform so that their decrees were peppered with exceptions that opened the back door to the same evils that the opening paragraphs excoriated.

Despite the overall failure of Lateran V, sincere reformers were involved in its deliberations. Giles of Viterbo (1469-1532), the Augustinian General, gave the memorable opening address to Lateran V which provided the watchword for Catholic reformers throughout the century: "Religion must change men; men may not change religion." Gifted in classical languages, Hebrew and Arabic, Giles shared Luther's antipathy for Aristotle and tried unsuccessfully to rebuild systematic theology on a Platonic base.

The model bishop of the early Catholic reformation was Gian Matteo Giberti (1495-1543) of Verona who carefully supervised the day to day activities of his priests, encouraging parish life by preaching, dignified worship, and a sense of brotherhood among parishioners. He founded orphanages and took up relief work for the poor, but he also subsidized scholars and set up a press to print religious literature for his people. Giberti's own life of prayer, frugality, preaching and study were the best advertisement for reform, but a flood of letters and his *Church Constitutions* spread his ideas through Italy and beyond the Alps.

The work of these reformers would have counted for little unless their spirit penetrated the highest church administrators. Paul III (1534-1549) was an unlikely candidate for a reform pope; created a cardinal at twenty-five by Alexander VI, he epitomized the decadence of Renaissance Rome, but Lateran V sparked a conversion so that at fifty-one he accepted ordination to the priesthood and reformed his life—or at least he put religion first since he never ceased to push the political interests of his family. Paul III continued the lavish papal patronage of the arts, notably Michelangelo's *Last Judgment;* even here the new spirit surfaced, for Paul questioned the ubiquitous nudes; Michelangelo replied by painting Paul among the damned with the ears of an ass and a serpent coiled around his body.

Perhaps Paul III's greatest contribution to reform was his choice of cardinals; political appointments continued as did nepotism, but the majority of the new cardinals were zealous churchmen who insured that coming popes would be reformers. Paul's greatest and most surprising choice of a cardinal was Gasparo Contarini. As a young noble Contarini had been the center of a circle of Venetian aristocrats who gathered for religious discussion. Several of them led by Paolo Guistiniani entered religious orders and became noteworthy reformers; but Contarini, who in 1511 underwent a religious conversion not unlike Luther's tower experience, determined to serve God and his city as a layman. Although he held the highest posts in the Venetian diplomatic service, he found time to write treatises on the immortality of the soul, the Venetian Constitution and a manual outlining the ideal bishop.

In 1536 Paul III put Contarini in charge of a committee to plan church reform. Paul must have cringed when he read their 1537 report, *Advice on Improving the Church.* "In the ordination of clerics, especially priests, no care is used, no diligence taken, so that unskilled men regardless of their low standing, bad habits and youth are admitted to sacred orders, even to the priesthood...whence flow numberless scandals, contempt for the clerical state and a lessening, even the destruction, of reverence for divine worship." "Visitors are scandalized when they enter St. Peter's basilica and find dirty, ignorant priests celebrating mass in vestments that would shame a poor parish." "Here in our city the prostitutes parade like matrons or ride on mules accompanied in broad daylight by clerics." The report also struck at papal greed and the purchase of dispensations and recommended the gradual suppression of corrupt religious orders. In all it specified twenty-six abuses for correction.

Paul lacked the courage to enforce the drastic proposals of the report, but he did try piecemeal reform. He authorized the Jesuits in 1540 and convoked the Council of Trent in 1545. Alarmed by pockets of Protestantism in Lucca and Modena, Paul instituted the Roman Inquisition in 1542. Never as severe as the Spanish Inquisition, the Roman Inquisition was confined to the Papal States, but the repression of heresy became more stringent everywhere in Italy.

Later popes were less compromising than Paul III; under the narrow minded Paul IV vagabond monks found themselves pulling an oar in the papal galleys. The splendor of the Renaissance disappeared and the exuberance of the Baroque lay far in the future. Life took on a militant, ascetic quality. Italian noblemen began wearing the black favored by Spanish grandees. Many Roman churches built in the decades after 1550 share an astringent simplicity and disciplined fervor with the music that Palestrina and Victoria were writing for their choirs. In religious art the anguished mannerism of Pantormo and the brutal realism of Caravaggio have one common characteristic, intensity. Here is how Rome in the 1570s impressed the English priest Gregory Martin:

> Being at Rome... in this time of Gregory XIII, and seeing there wonderful variety of blessed monuments, of devout persons, of godly and charitable exercises from day to day never ceasing; the churches, the martyrs, the glorious ashes of undoubted saints, the places where they prayed, preached, fasted, were imprisoned, died; when I saw moreover the good examples of all degrees, the preaching, teaching, confessing, communicating, visiting of holy places,... kneeling, knocking, sighing, weeping, creeping,

all other manner of fervent, comely and unfeigned devotion; when I saw the alms, the religious houses, the hospitals, the colleges, the seminaries, the merciful and bountiful provision for all kind of poor and needy persons; when I saw for this purpose the confraternities and congregations, so many, so honorable, so careful of all deeds of mercy and good works. And (that which is a great cause of all the rest) when I saw the majesty of the see apostolic, his holiness among his cardinals, as Michael among the angels,...their solemnity in chapel, their wisdom in consistory, audience at home and in their chambers, courtesy in all places mixed with great discretion,...I was in a manner rapt besides myself with admiration thereof, and said within myself very much like as [the Queen of Sheba] said to [Solomon]. It is a very true report which I have heard and read of this noble city; I did scarce think it credible till myself came and saw it with mine eyes and found that the half part was not told me.

Catholic spirituality teaches not only man's individual relationship directly to God but also his union with his fellow man in working out his salvation. Through the centuries this conviction gave rise to a baffling variety of associations and confraternities which combined corporate worship, public charity and good fellowship. The medieval guilds combined all these with the functions of a modern trade union; the guilds did not disappear in early modern times but their stagnation allowed new organizations to take over many of their functions.

The best studied lay confraternities of the Catholic reformation are the *Scuole* of Venice, which grew from medieval flagellant clubs. Venice had over one hundred confraternities, but lay religion centered on the five great *Scuole* whose six thousand members in 1575 counted about ten percent of the adult males. Public flagellation, their most spectacular activity, was in fact subordinate to other functions. They had a military role since they provided a ready reserve for the fleet; more importantly, their prestigious offices were reserved for ordinary citizens, an important compensation for their exclusion from political power in Venice, where a narrow nobility monopolized state offices. Priests served as chaplains but had no voice in governing the *Scuole*. The *Scuole* brothers marched and worshiped together on festivals; even humble members could count on an impressive funeral with long ranks of the brothers following his coffin. The sense of brotherhood reached beyond the grave because the *Scuole* offered prayers and masses for dead members. Each confraternity had its headquarters, massive piles which overshadowed the palazzos of the nobility. The greatest series of late Renaissance paintings is Tintoretto's biblical cycle at the Scuola di San Rocco, where sixty-seven of them still hang. Many of these Tintoretto undertook free of charge as an act of devotion, but also as a tribute to his fellow members at San Rocco.

The most important function of the *Scuole* was public charity. Enrollment carefully balanced rich and poor members. The *Scuole* were well endowed by gifts and legacies from rich members; poor members had first claim on these resources, but after their needs had been met, alms were distributed to the "deserving poor" according to intelligent, discriminating planning. After alms, dowries were the most important charity, followed by medical help, especially in the famous hospitals for the incurable victims of syphilis, then a virulent new scourge.

The Council of Trent

Throughout church history ecumenical councils have traditionally dealt with doctrinal crises. As early as 1518 Martin Luther appealed from papal judgment to a future ecumenical council, and in the next decades both Protestants and Catholics repeated this call, although they disagreed about the proper makeup and authority of the council. Clement VII, fearing recrudescent conciliarism, made excuses to Charles V for not calling a council, but Paul III promised a council shortly after his election. War and threats of war between Francis I and Charles V prevented its meeting until 1545. Even then recurrent tensions between France, the emperor and the pope broke its sessions into three periods, 1545-1547, 1552-1553, and 1562-1563. Attendance was never large (between 32 and 228 bishops), and Italians always constituted the majority. Bishops found many excuses for not coming. Trent, nestled in the Alps between Italy and the Empire, was small, inconvenient, and expensive. Bishops from northern Europe who faced crises at home feared to go to a council that seemed to drag on forever. During most of the sessions the French kings as part of their rivalry with the Hapsburgs prevented their bishops from attending. Only the bishops and five heads of religious orders were allowed to vote, but many theologians contributed to the preliminary discussions. Debate was free enough. One bishop defended a Lutheran theory of justification, and another bishop became so impassioned that he yanked a fistful of hair from a colleague's beard.

The monarchs were represented by ambassadors; Charles V was particularly influential since he could count on the support of bishops from Spain, Naples, Sicily and Milan. At the outset the Emperor wanted to restrict discussion to church reform—he opposed doctrinal definitions because they would cut down his room to negotiate with the German Protestants. The papal legates wanted to define Catholic teaching on the points raised by the Protestant reformers. All the major Protestant groups had worked out official creeds and statements on the disputed issues, whereas Catholics had a general tradition but no defined statement of dogma. This left laymen confused and put Catholic controversialists at a disadvantage; only an ecumenical council could clear the air by defining Catholic teaching. Eventually representatives of the pope and the emperor struck a compromise to discuss doctrine and reform together. Trent never tried to produce a balanced statement of all Catholic doctrine but contented itself with the issues raised by the Reformation crisis. Generally the council confirmed medieval theology, but it avoided the technical vocabulary of scholasticism and tried to remain neutral on points disputed by Catholic schools of thought.

On justification Trent steered a course between Pelagius and Luther. It condemned the Pelagian view that man can be justified by his own works without the grace of Christ: man needs grace to believe, hope, love, repent and find justification. "We are therefore said to be freely justified because nothing that precedes justification, whether faith or works, merits the grace of justification." On the other hand Trent asserted against Luther that man's free will, moved and aroused by God, can co-operate in preparing itself for justification. Man's will is not inanimate and passive but can resist grace. Trent refused to regard all acts before justification as true sins. Once justified by God's freely given grace, man can merit an increase in grace. Trent denied that man, short of a special revelation, can know with certitude whether or not he is predestined.

On the problem of the criteria of religious knowledge Trent insisted that the church has the power to interpret the meaning of scripture and that tradition has authority with the Bible. Trent, following the Council of Florence, continued to include Tobit, Judith, Sirach, the Wisdom of Solomon and the two books of Maccabees in its list of the books of the Bible.

The council also affirmed that Christ instituted seven sacraments: baptism, the eucharist, penance, confirmation, marriage, orders, and the final anointing. Their objective power to confer grace does not depend upon the holiness of the recipient or of the minister. Infants can validly receive baptism. "Christ, true God and man is truly, really, and substantially contained" in the eucharist; accordingly the host may be adored publicly and privately. At mass, which is a true sacrifice, the eucharist may be received under the appearance of bread alone. Trent also reaffirmed the existence of purgatory but warned preachers about treating its abstruse aspects which do not foster piety. In a guarded decree the council condemned those who say indulgences are worthless, but it abolished the office of indulgence peddling. The council urged the faithful to call on the saints for help and approved the use of sacred art.

Trent issued no decree on the nature of the church or papal authority (these subjects had to wait for Vatican I and II); but the council turned over to the pope several unfinished projects: issuing a catechism and an index of forbidden books, standardizing the missal, and supervising a new Latin Bible. These tasks and the ability shown by the popes and their legates in carrying the council through to completion increased papal prestige. Paradoxically the bishops also gained power at Trent because its regulations laid on them the main task of reform and curtailed the frequent papal dispensations which had previously undermined episcopal authority.

The council passed nearly two hundred pages of legislation which tried to uproot long standing abuses such as appointing relatives to church incomes, holding several bishoprics simultaneously, and laymen holding church offices for the sake of their income. Most of the legislation dealt with churchmen—the election of bishops and religious superiors, chapter duties, annual diocesan synods, preaching, entering and leaving convents and the like. Some legislation touched the laity, thus secret weddings were declared invalid and marriage regulations much simplified; those engaged in duels and their seconds incur excommunication and forfeit their property. Some regulations are mere exhortation: cardinals and bishops must have plain furniture and keep a plain table; other laws have teeth: priests who keep concubines are first to be deprived of their income, then excommunicated, then imprisoned until they reform.

The most important measures dealt with the training of

priests. To prevent the swarms of untrained priests without pastoral duties that had cursed the medieval church, Trent declared that candidates must be twenty-five, carefully trained, and must be assigned pastoral duties together with sufficient income. Bishops may not ordain for payment. Henceforward there were to be fewer but better priests. Trent ordered every diocese to open a seminary and laid down a step by step training. Obviously this reform took hold slowly and had drawbacks, for it withdrew priests from the universities and the mainstream of European intellectual life, thereby increasing clerical inbreeding, but the gain outweighed the loss. Trent also tackled the problem of absentee bishops and priests by linking income to residence. So great was this problem that at any given time there might be a hundred bishops in Rome hunting around for ecclesiastical plums or just bored with their sleepy cathedral towns.

St. Charles Borromeo (1538-1584) showed how important residence was. When he turned his back on curial Rome, he became the first archbishop to reside in Milan for eighty years. His presence, attentive to detail, emaciated by prayer and fasting, personally attending the plague victims, galvanized his priests and people into reform. Borromeo also carried through Trent's decree that bishops visit regularly every parish under them. The record of his pastoral visitations (edited in several scholarly volumes by a young priest who became John XXIII) gives a good picture of reform at the grass roots. Perhaps Borromeo's greatest contribution was founding the Confraternity of Christian Doctrine, the forerunner of the Sunday school, which soon enrolled 40,000 students in 740 schools throughout his vast archdiocese. Only a step behind Borromeo was the work of Cardinal Gabriele Paleotti at Bologna and many others. Without their inspiration the legislation of Trent would have remained mere paper.

To what extent was the Catholic reformation a reaction to Protestantism? The dogmatic decrees of Trent were obviously directed against Protestantism, as were the index of forbidden books and the Inquisition, but the moral and spiritual renewal owed little to the rise of Protestantism. Catholics in those countries most threatened by Protestantism seemed lethargic compared to reformers in Italy and Spain, which were more insulated. Most of the major Catholic reformers committed themselves to action independent of any Protestant impulse. Indeed, the rise of Protestantism may have retarded certain reforms: a Latin liturgy, only the most obvious example, was perhaps defensible in the age of Erasmus when Latin was the common patrimony of the educated and the national languages were still in their formative period, often split into many dialects; by the end of the sixteenth century Latin was outmoded, and three centuries later it was ridiculous, but the Catholic church continued its use partly from sheer tradition, partly from an all-too-human contrariness, since the Protestant reformers had staked their claim to the vernaculars.

The New Orders

On May 20, 1520, French artillery battered the walls of Pamplona and the infantry surged through the breach. Among the captured Spaniards was the Basque hidalgo Ignatius of Loyola (1491-1556), his right leg smashed by a cannon ball. Twice the broken bone was set, and to wile away the convalescence at the family castle, Ignatius asked for romances of chivalry, but the only books available were the lives of Christ and the saints. In them Loyola discovered a new kind of heroism which warmed his heart more than his usual daydreams of knightly exploits. Loyola determined to match the saints in heroism and started for Jerusalem as soon as he recovered his strength. After dedicating his life to God at the famous monastery-shrine of Monserrat, he stopped at the nearby village of Manresa for a few days of prayer. The days lengthened to eleven months of fasting, penance and prayer. At times he was close to despair and suicide, but finally he achieved peace after a series of mystical experiences. At the price of begging several questions, mysticism can be defined as the direct, immediate experience different from ordinary sense perception or reasoning, of an object perceived as ultimate. Historians, who can judge mystical encounter (private and ineffable of its nature) only from its results, have no reason to doubt Loyola's claim that the Manresa experiences gave peace and purpose to his life.

In a ragged notebook Loyola kept an account of these experiences and from them distilled his *Spiritual Exercises*, published in 1548, one of the strangest and most influential books in history. Largely written before the author acquired a formal education, the *Exercises* depend only in a general way on earlier spiritual literature. The casual reader will find the *Exercises* a confusing cluster of Chinese boxes; like a cookbook or a manual on body-building, the value of the *Exercises* can be judged only by doing, not by reading. The book outlines for directors a thirty-day series of religious practices and meditations, mainly on the life of Christ, designed to help Christians dedicate themselves to God-centered living. The *Exercises* are clear, precise, and vivid; above all they reveal a profound understanding of religious psychology and possess a unique power to transform lives. In them Loyola shares in a lower, ascetical key the thrust of his mystical experiences.

The *Exercises* also teach techniques of systematic mental prayer so that the exercitant learns to apply his memory, imagination, reason and will to biblical accounts and his personal problems. Loyola's techniques for systematic prayer carry forward medieval practices; later writers worked out similar techniques. The spread of daily meditation probably contributed more than all the decrees of Trent to greater holiness among Catholic priests, nuns and devout lay people. Meditation manuals had considerable vogue also among Protestants.

On his return from Jerusalem, Loyola realized that his ignorance limited his effectiveness as an apostle. Accordingly he joined grammar school classes at Barcelona to get enough Latin to understand university lectures. While he was a student at the Universities of Alcalá and Salamanca, the Inquisition arrested him; after interrogation the inquisitors admitted his orthodoxy but forbade his street preaching and spiritual counselling. He refused to accept these restrictions and transferred to the University of Paris where he spent the years from 1528 to 1535 in the study of Aristotle and Thomistic theology. He greatly admired the orderliness of the Paris system and copied it later in his nascent Jesuit colleges.

Loyola had an extraordinary gift for friendship and for discerning men who could do great things for God. Despite initial hesitancy he gradually won over several fellow students to his ideals, largely by conducting them through the *Spiritual Exercises*. After a long journey home to restore his health and settle his affairs, he rejoined his companions at Venice in January, 1537. The group was international from the start: four Spaniards, two Savoyards, two Frenchmen, and a Portuguese; except for one who died shortly, all of them became distinguished preachers, theologians, administrators or missionaries.

Their goal was to serve as missionaries to the Moslems in Palestine. While awaiting passage they worked at the most menial jobs in the Venetian hospitals; only at this juncture did Loyola and most of the others accept ordination. When war between Venice and the Turks ruled out travel to Palestine, the companions went to Rome and put their services at the pope's disposal, but gradually they realized that only the formal structure of a religious order could cement their companionship in God's service. Loyola summarized their months of discussion in an outline of the future constitutions of the Society of Jesus, which he submitted to Paul III. At Contarini's urging the pope approved these late in 1540. Loyola was elected superior general by every vote except his own.

During the next few years the first Jesuits scattered, some

as papal nuncios to Ireland and Germany, others as preachers in the Italian cities, others as professors in Rome and Bavaria. Francis Xavier went to India and began the greatest missionary career since the Apostles, while Simon Rodriguez founded the flourishing Portuguese province.

Loyola spent his last sixteen years in Rome as superior general, directing by letter the far-flung activities of his brothers. Nearly seven thousand letters from his last eight years are extant and reveal a man of enormous zeal and practicality. During these years he also dictated a short autobiography which indicates that the mystical experiences, largely dormant during his student years, came flooding back. Loyola was that rarest figure, the mystic as bureaucrat. His greatest accomplishment during the Roman years was the *Constitutions of the Society of Jesus.* Four centuries of Jesuit history suggest that Loyola was a masterful legislator, for Jesuit internal history has been remarkably placid—no major splinter movements, no upheavals, only gradual adaptation to changing times. In writing his constitutions Loyola studied past models, but he introduced important changes. The Jesuits are the most centralized religious order, mainly because a single superior general elected for life appoints all important superiors. The Jesuits dispensed with many monastic customs—no obligatory penances, no special habit, no singing of the divine office, no stability vowed to a particular house or province. Any Jesuit can be moved anywhere in the world. Having stripped off much monastic protection, Loyola compensated by rigorous admission standards and prolonged training. His aim was to mold the contemplative in action, the apostle whose prayer fires his work and whose work feeds his prayer. In those areas where Loyola broke with the practice of the earlier monks and friars, later orders followed or went beyond him; indeed, many older orders modified their life style in practice to make it more effective for apostolic action.

Loyola wanted quality rather than numbers, but the Jesuits

grew rapidly; by his death in 1556 there were a thousand, by 1615 thirteen thousand. Foreign missions became the preferred Jesuit apostolate; by Loyola's death there were Jesuit missions to Brazil, the Congo, Ethiopia, India, Indonesia and Japan. Today seven thousand Jesuits serve as missionaries. From 1546 to 1550 the Jesuits founded twelve colleges, first for their own members, then for lay students; gradually education became their most important apostolate, with 372 colleges by 1615. Most of these colleges corresponded to present day preparatory schools but some were full-fledged universities. Jesuit education took the humanist curriculum of the Renaissance, purified it and simplified it. The Jesuits codified their early experiments in *The Plan of Studies* of 1599, which laid down a step by step program so that students knew where they were and could see their progress. Class attendance was compulsory and friendly rivalry replaced the rod in motivating students.

Perhaps the best index of Catholic vitality has been the foundation of religious orders and congregations. Religious life, based on vows of poverty, chastity and obedience and committed to communal living, has proven most adaptable. Religious orders arise from religious needs at the grass roots level; the papacy approves religious orders but never founds them. Sixteenth-century Italy provides a classic example. A doctor, a lawyer and a professor of mathematics founded the Barnabites at Milan in 1537 to deal with the sufferings of war, poverty and plague. Concurrently an ex-soldier started the Somaschi near Bergamo to look after orphans and plague victims. The low level of parish life prompted the founding of the Theatines in 1524; more austere and aristocratic than the Jesuits, they remained few in numbers but cultivated an intense devotional life. Their background made them a seedbed of reforming bishops.

Reforming old orders involved more difficulties than founding new ones. Bishops and general superiors who sent in outsiders to reform a lax monastery were sure to encounter resentment. One group tried to assassinate Charles Borromeo for his efforts. Another pattern was for nuns or friars who wanted a stricter life to form a splinter group. This pattern also caused tensions, both because it seemed to insult the parent group and because it usually drew off the most fervent members. The early history of the Capuchin order illustrates these tensions. The Franciscans were already split into Conventuals and the stricter Observants when several young friars felt called to a literal interpretation of the Franciscan rule. Some tried to work within the Observant framework, but others led by Matteo da Bascio obtained papal permission for a more solitary life style. They built simple hermitages on the outskirts of Italian towns where they lived in absolute poverty and devoted themselves to prayer. But they also ventured into the cities to beg their bread, to care for the sick and poor, and to preach on street corners in a homely, popular style. In their desire for simplicity, they let their beards grow and adopted a coarse four-pointed hood patterned after St. Francis; this distinctive *cappuccio* gave them their name. The Capuchin life style proved popular in Italy, especially among the lower classes; unfortunately it also attracted too many young Observant Franciscans. Inevitably both Observants and Capuchins appealed to the pope and lined up support. Paul III nearly suppressed the Capuchins in 1542 after their general, Bernardino Ochino, fled to Geneva; but an examination of Capuchin preachers vindicated their orthodoxy. By 1550 there were 2,500 friars in Italy, and after 1572 they spread across the Alps, particularly to France. Eventually the Capuchins proved the most influential of the new orders aside from the Jesuits.

Mysticism

The sixteenth century was Spain's golden age, but ultimately her power waned because she failed to develop a system of manufacture and commerce equal to the overseas empire that her soldiers, governors and missionaries built abroad. Even though the Dutch and English surpassed Spain as colonial powers in the seventeenth century, Spain and Portugal (which was united to Spain during the crucial years 1580 to 1640) laid the foundations of Latin American civilization in religion, language and culture.

Striking as were the exploits of Cortes, Pizarro and Coronado, other Spaniards were exploring realms more distant and difficult. The reign of Philip II was the golden age of Spanish mysticism. To many Christians the mystic appears as impractical and withdrawn, as having little interest in sacraments, public worship, the institutional church or traditional theology. The Spanish mystics of the sixteenth century refute all these clichés. Most of them were warm human beings of shrewd common sense who worked hard to forward the good of the church. Several were great writers as well. Harnessing their spiritual energy to institutional needs may be the greatest accomplishment of the Catholic reformation.

The greatest Spanish prose writer of the century was Luis de Leon (1527-1591), an Augustinian friar and one of the last Renaissance men. Learned in canon law, philosophy, mathematics and half a dozen languages, he was primarily a student of scripture and scholastic theology, which he taught at the University of Salamanca. His greatest books are *The Perfect Marriage*, a spiritual guide for husbands and wives, and *The Names of Christ*, which uses the framework of a Platonic dialogue to examine all the titles which the Old and New Testaments apply to Christ. His prose style tries to adapt Ciceronian clarity and elevation to Spanish. His lyric poetry moves from the contemplation of beauty in nature and music to the yearning for mystical union with God. A slashing lecturer with little patience for pedantic colleagues, Luis made many enemies and ran afoul of the Inquisition. Exonerated after four years in prison, he took up his lectures ironically: "As I was saying yesterday...."

Fray Luis also wrote a popular biography of St. Teresa of

Avila (1515-1582), but for interest it cannot compare with her own autobiography. Thanks to her writings, we can know Teresa more intimately than any other person of her century; only Montaigne comes close to her in unfolding his psychological processes, and he is neither so candid nor so great-souled. Her style is clear and spontaneous, dignified but free of literary artifice.

The life of a cloistered Carmelite nun might seem uneventful, but hers certainly was not. The greatest events were within, for she scaled the height of mystical contemplation, which she describes in both personal and theoretic terms. Far from withdrawing to cherish her encounters with God, she determined to reform the Carmelite order. Her project met opposition not only from nuns content with mediocrity but from tumultuous public meetings and law suits. She passed her last twenty years in endless journeys across the baked plateau of Castile from one reformed convent to another, exhorting nuns, persuading bishops, dickering with nuncios; even Philip II became caught up in the controversy. In the end her tact, buoyancy and holiness prevailed.

The life of her confessor, St. John of the Cross (1542-1591), makes even clearer the animosities aroused by the reform. John started the first reformed community of Carmelite friars in 1568. Seven years later Carmelites opposed to the new movement kidnapped John and imprisoned him for nine months in a tiny cell where they tried to break his spirit by psychological torture, weekly scourgings and half-starvation. Stripped of all, John possessed all; and his Visitor gave him a food of which his jailers knew not. Eventually he escaped the monastery prison by lowering a chain of blankets through a window. The poems on which his literary reputation rests center on these months; modelled on the Song of Solomon, they describe his mystical experiences in the pastoral setting so beloved by Renaissance poets. Lacking the bonhomie of St. Teresa, John of the Cross more than compensates by precise, orderly exposition, the fruit of his training in scholastic theology at Salamanca. His prose treatises are elaborate commentaries on his poetry; thus his *The Ascent of Mount Carmel* explains "The Dark Night." Other works describe the heights of mystical experience.

France settled her war with Spain in 1598, the same year that the Edict of Nantes brought internal religious peace. The French Catholic church then entered a period of rapid development just when Italy and Spain began to lose their spiritual élan. St. Francis de Sales (1567-1622) was the greatest spiritual writer of the French school. As a young priest he served in the Chablais, a Calvinist district near Geneva but under the jurisdiction of Savoy. Gradually his zeal, gentleness and skill in controversy, together with the support of the Duke of Savoy, won over most of the region. In 1602 he was consecrated bishop of Geneva, but his ministry was restricted to the outlying districts since the city retained its Calvinist heritage. His *Introduction to the Devout Life*, published in 1608, had enormous success; within fifty years it was available in eighteen languages and countless editions. Spanish mystical writers aimed at contemplative monks and nuns; St. Francis aimed his book at all Christians (especially lay women of the leisured classes). He took the methods of Loyola and simplified and adapted them to a wider audience. His teaching is always clear, flexible, gentle and practical; usually he reinforces it through homely examples and similes.

St. Francis laid stress on the need for spiritual direction in both his books and his letters. Many holy women sought his guidance, most notably St. Jane Frances de Chantal with whom he founded the Visitation Order for women whose health did not permit great austerity but who desired a life of prayer and active charity. The order expanded rapidly—eighty-six houses in its first twenty-one years—but later a "male chauvinist" archbishop forced them into strict cloister and cut off their active works.

A generation later in 1663 St. Vincent de Paul and St. Louise de Marillac broke through this narrowminded opposition by founding the Daughters of Charity to care for the poor and the sick. To circumvent squeamish churchmen, they avoided solemn vows, recruited country girls used to hard work, and clothed their sisters in a grey habit modelled on peasant dress. Napoleon, who had seen their work among his wounded, once cut short a eulogy of the new enlightened philanthropy: "All well and good, gentlemen, but give us a Grey Sister anytime." Without the Daughters of Charity and the dozens of active congregations of sisters who followed after them, modern Catholicism is scarcely conceivable.

8

Wider Horizons

Reformation in Eastern Europe

During the sixteenth century Poland-Lithuania was the largest state in Christendom, and Polish tradition considers the era its golden century. Sigismund I (1506-1548) sought peace to foster internal growth, but since his lands stretched nearly to the Black Sea, he could not avoid border warfare with Ivan the Terrible. In Poland the Reformation coincided with the Renaissance. Poland cultivated its ties with Italy, which Sigismund strengthened by marrying Bona Sforza of Milan. Copernicus, the greatest Pole of the era, studied at both Cracow and Padua. Despite its high culture, Poland was not a strong centralized state. Its union with Lithuania was largely dynastic, and six languages were spoken within their borders. Powerful nobles dominated outlying districts everywhere and controlled the parliament. Polish kings might set policy but their weak bureaucracy depended on the co-operation of the nobles and gentry. The cities contained large colonies of German merchants.

Lutheran ideas spread to Poland as early as 1518, especially among the merchants and young nobles returning from the German universities. Sigismund I issued an edict against Lutheran books but refrained from active persecution; indeed, there was almost no persecution in Poland during the sixteenth century. By mid-century Calvinists

matched Lutherans in influence; not only did Anabaptists
find toleration, but even various anti-trinitarian views,
propagated mainly by refugee Italians, flourished. The high
tide of Polish Protestantism came with the Diet of Piotrkow
of 1565 which restricted the jurisdiction of church courts and
thereby allowed nobles to establish Protestantism on their
estates. Sigismund II (1548-1572), who corresponded with
Melanchthon and Calvin, was on excellent terms with his
Protestant subjects.

Why did Protestantism fail to capture Poland? It never
took deep root among the peasantry who constituted the
bulk of the nation. The very multiplicity of denominations
led to ceaseless infighting. Moreover, Polish Protestantism
failed to produce a leader of real stature and failed to win
over the monarchy. Kings Stephen Bathory (1576-1586) and
Sigismund III (1587-1632) supported the counter reformation
and encouraged the Jesuits who began their work in Poland
in 1564. Since the Jesuit schools were the best in Poland,
many Protestant nobles enrolled their sons; the sons returned
as Catholics and later led their peasants back to the old faith.

The leading Polish churchman, Cardinal Stanislaus Hosius
(1504-1579) exerted a strong influence for reform among his
fellow bishops and waged an unremitting pamphlet war
against the Protestants. A new breed of priests from his
seminaries carried on his work. No less influential was the
Jesuit Peter Skarga (1536-1612) who like Hosius studied both
at Cracow and in Italy. On returning to Poland, he taught
theology and wrote polemics defending Catholic teaching.
Concurrently he founded or enlarged seven Jesuit colleges
plus a host of charitable brotherhoods in the larger Polish
cities. For twenty-four years he was court preacher to
Sigismund III; his sermons not only marked a milestone in
the development of Polish literature and national conscious-
ness but strongly influenced national policy.

Poland had more Ukrainian (Ruthenian) Orthodox subjects than Protestants. As Skarga never ceased pointing out,

their reunion with Rome (based on the agreements reached at the Council of Florence) would wed them more firmly to Poland and detach them from Muscovy. From the point of view of Rome and Warsaw Skarga made good sense, but his arguments also evoked a genuine response among the Ruthenian nobles and bishops. Indeed, contact with Protestantism tended to show Orthodox and Catholics how much they had in common. In 1590 the Metropolitan of Kiev convened a synod of Ruthenians which approved a request for union with Rome. After several years of discussion among Orthodox and Catholics, the union proposals were ratified by a majority of the Orthodox bishops at the Synod of Brest in 1596. Several bishops who opposed the union were deposed, giving rise to bitter resentment. The Ruthenians kept their own liturgy, calendar and customs but acknowledged papal primacy; gradually, however, many Ruthenians came to feel like second-class citizens in the predominately Latin church and returned to Orthodoxy. Meanwhile an even more glittering prospect arose before Polish Catholicism— nothing less than the religious-political conquest of Russia.

If sixteenth-century Poland was sprawling and decentralized compared to England and France, what can be said of Russia? Menaced on the south by the Turks, on the west by the Poles and Swedes, on the east by the Tartars, Russia's borders were blurred and fluctuating. Much of the population (estimates range from four to seventeen million) was migratory. In theory the czar claimed absolute power by divine right; in practice the noble boyars controlled the rudimentary administration. The first Czar, Ivan the Terrible (1533-1584), tried to catapult Russia forward by terror and sheer will. His wars against the Tartars led to dramatic eastward expansion, but Poland and Sweden defeated his drive to the Baltic. To circumvent the boyar-controlled administration, Ivan set up his new reform officials, the *Oprichniki*, who were really private terror squads. Living on confiscated estates and dressed entirely in black, they ranged forth on black horses to carry out the czar's whim. Paranoid and sadistic, Ivan murdered tens of thousands of Russians. He massacred the citizens of Novgorod on a rumor of disloyalty. Nobody was safe; Ivan sewed the archbishop of Novgorod into a bearskin and threw him to the hounds.

In general, Ivan treated churchmen like servants to be used and discarded; from 1563 to 1571 he ran through five metropolitans of Moscow. His piety was consistent with his twisted character. He loved to compose monastic rules and plan elaborate liturgical ceremonies, but like his contemporary Henry III of France he alternated hours of religious devotions with sexual orgies. Ivan tried half-heartedly to reform the Orthodox church by holding a council in 1551 which condemned a catalogue of clerical abuses—illiteracy, drunkenness, debauchery—but the council became bogged down in liturgical details (should the sign of the cross be made with two fingers or three?) and accomplished little. More important, councils in 1547 and 1549 pushed through an unprecedented canonization of thirty-nine Russian saints; this was Holy Russia's counterblast to Trent and Rome, to Wittenberg and Geneva, even to the patriarch of Constantinople.

Ivan's crowning villainy was killing his eldest son in a fit of rage. His own death shortly later began Russia's famous Time of Troubles. Ivan left two sons, the imbecile Theodore and the infant Dimitri who died mysteriously in 1591. Theodore's reign (1584-1598) was dominated by his brother-in-law Boris Godunov, who then succeeded him as czar. Boris quickly lost his early popularity and began to suspect boyar plots everywhere; his suspicions forced the boyars to concert real plots. Meanwhile an impostor arose who claimed to be Ivan's youngest son Dimitri. In Poland the false Dimitri converted to Catholicism and gathered an army of cossacks and Polish adventurers to invade Russia. Dimitri played his role so well that not even his bad generalship kept the Russians from flocking to his banner. The sudden death of Boris

Godunov opened the gates of Moscow. Having acquired a kingdom by his wits, Dimitri rushed to enjoy it, little heeding that his entourage of Jesuits and his indifference to Orthodox ceremonies were alienating his people. Amid riots instigated by the boyars an assassin struck down Dimitri in the Kremlin in May, 1606. Russia collapsed into anarchy, torn between a second false Dimitri, a feeble czar, and ravaging cossacks from the Don and Volga.

Meanwhile Sigismund III of Poland readied his army and waited. In 1609 he launched a Polish Catholic crusade. One army beseiged Smolensk, another smashed a larger Russian army and entered Moscow in September, 1610. At first Sigismund guaranteed Orthodoxy and proposed his son as czar; but after the occupation of Moscow he revealed his plan to foster Catholicism and unite Russia and Poland under his rule. To defend Mother Russia and Orthodoxy the hostile Russian factions sank their differences; one Russian army starved out the Polish garrison in the Kremlin while others turned back the Polish relief columns. In February, 1613, Michael Romanov was elected czar, the first of the dynasty that was to rule Russia until 1917. The Catholic reformation had its greatest triumph in Poland, but its defeat at Moscow in 1612 ensured that Catholicism and Orthodoxy would share Slavic Europe.

The religious history of the Czechs, Slovaks, Croatians and Hungarians paralleled that of the Poles. Throughout eastern Europe German merchants were the first to spread Luther's ideas. In Bohemia, Lutheranism easily linked up with the native Hussite tradition. By mid-century Calvinism was spreading at the expense of Lutheranism, particularly among the Hungarians. Despite favorable beginnings Protestantism ended as an isolated minority in all these nations. The spread of Jesuit colleges played the same role as in Poland. More important, all these lands were partially under the Catholic Hapsburgs who gradually tightened their control, sometimes by outright persecutions, usually by more subtle pressures that won first the nobles and then their peasants back to Catholicism. In Hungary, Protestants had good reason to prefer the Turks to the less tolerant Hapsburgs; conversely the Turks tended to favor Protestants over Catholics. Nevertheless the Catholic reformation followed the slow advance of Hapsburg arms down the Danube.

The Thirty Years War

The Thirty Years War is a title of convenience which was invented later to describe a series of wars which centered on Germany during the first half of the seventeenth century. In fact the fighting spilled over the traditional thirty years (1618-1648) and involved all Europe from Lisbon to Smolensk. For the Swedes the war was a glorious episode in their hundred year struggle for dominion of the Baltic. For the Spaniards and the Dutch it was part of the eighty years war of Dutch independence. For France it marked a major victory in her efforts to break out of the Hapsburg ring of territories which went back to Charles V.

The German aspect of the war began in 1618 when the Bohemian Protestant nobility staged a *coup d'état* at Prague against their newly elected king, the Hapsburg archduke Ferdinand. They saw that Ferdinand, a militant Catholic, was bent on undermining their traditional rights and religious liberty. The Bohemians then invited Elector Frederick of the Palatine, a dashing but inept Calvinist, to be their king. The Lutheran princes stood aloof when Frederick tried to invade Austria. Ferdinand meanwhile secured his election as Emperor and gathered his forces from the Hapsburg crown lands, from Spain and from the German Catholic League led by Maximilian of Bavaria. After an hour's fight at the White Mountain Ferdinand marched into Prague and began to purge the Bohemian nobility, distributing their lands to his supporters. Meanwhile Spanish and Bavarian troops occupied the Palatinate.

In 1625 Christian IV entered the war to expand his German holdings and shore up the Protestant cause. During the turmoil many armies deteriorated into marauding bands who pillaged friend and foe alike. For these religion and politics mattered little; war became a way of life and an end in itself. The generals were often adventurers trying to carve out a personal estate. The greatest of these was Wallenstein, who reduced pillage and requisition to a self-sustaining system. His mercenaries and the army of the Catholic League easily smashed Christian IV and occupied much of northern Germany. Heady with success, Emperor Ferdinand in 1629 demanded that the Protestant princes give up all the church lands they had absorbed since 1552. This extreme demand was a mistake, for it drove the princes to desperation, started a scramble for land among the victorious Catholics, and alarmed France.

For Cardinal Richelieu, the director of French policy, the glory of France and the humbling of the Hapsburgs were more important than a Catholic triumph in Germany. Having settled with England and the Huguenots, he prepared for French intervention in Germany. First he tried to control the Swiss passes through which Spain fed troops into Germany and the Netherlands; then he paid King Gustavus Adolphus of Sweden to take up the Protestant crusade after Christian IV had failed.

Gustavus was a curious mixture of religious zeal and *Realpolitik*; undoubtedly he saw himself as the saviour of German Lutheranism, but the deliberations of the royal council and his propaganda in Sweden stressed the domination of the Baltic and Swedish security as the reasons for intervention. His army was not large but had no equal in equipment, training and morale. At first Gustavus moved slowly to secure his bases on the German coast, but once joined by Protestant Saxony and Brandenburg he invaded central Germany and defeated the imperial army. The emperor had to recall Wallenstein from disfavor. Near Leipzig in 1632

Gustavus defeated Wallenstein's mercenaries but died on the field. Shortly afterwards Emperor Ferdinand had Wallenstein executed for treason. The war dragged on since the Swedes could not conquer the Catholic south nor could the imperial generals dislodge them from northern Germany.

A stalemate hardly fitted Richelieu's plan to cripple Hapsburg power; accordingly France had to intervene directly in Germany and the Spanish Netherlands. The last phase of the war (1635-1648) pitted Catholic France, aided by Sweden, against the Emperor and Spain. Perhaps the decisive events were revolts against Philip IV in Portugal and Catalonia. Although the Thrity Years War is often considered a religious war, religion was subordinate to politics. The Peace of Westphalia of 1648 ended the fighting in the Empire, but war between France and Spain continued for eleven more years. France and Sweden gained stretches of German territory and a continuing voice in imperial affairs. Brandenburg, Saxony and Bavaria also made territorial gains. The war marked the last serious attempt to control Germany by the Hapsburg emperors, who now turned their energies toward Austria and southeastern expansion against the Turks. Significantly the papal nuncios were excluded from important negotiations, and papal protests were ignored. Henceforward religion was to be kept separate from international politics, although the union of church and state remained everywhere the norm. The peace treaty granted Calvinism legal recognition with Lutheranism and Catholicism. The treaty also put minor restrictions on the right of princes to determine the religion of their states: they had to tolerate established minorities and could not confiscate the property of religious exiles.

By the Peace of Westphalia the drive of both the Protestant and Catholic reformations was played out. Scandinavia and northern Germany were solidly Lutheran. Calvinism dominated Switzerland, Scotland, Holland and several German principalities. Anglicanism was the main religion of

England, but the Puritan Revolution of 1642 brought to the fore many groups of Protestant dissenters.

Two-thirds of western and central Europe remained Catholic. The Latin nations—Italy, Spain, Portugal and France—were solidly Catholic. Catholics dominated southern Germany and were strong in the Rhineland. Ireland and the Spanish Netherlands were Catholic outposts in northern Europe. In Eastern Europe the Russians, Romanians and the southern Slavs remained loyal to Eastern Orthodoxy, while the Poles, Czechs, Slovaks, Croats and the Slovenes were mostly Catholic. The religious lines of Europe remained remarkably stable after 1648 until the industrial revolution and modern war began massive shifts of population.

Christianity the World Over

If a visitor from outer space had tried in the late fifteenth century to assess the future of various religions and cultures, he surely would have not given first place to Christianity, which was mainly confined to the European peninsula of the great Eurasian land mass. Perhaps he would have chosen Islam, which early had nourished a great culture. Islam was still advancing in Black Africa, India, Indonesia and on the Tartar steppes. The Ottoman Turks had recently conquered Constantinople and ended a thousand years of Byzantine civilization. The Sultan surpassed any Christian ruler in power, and his armies were steadily subduing the Balkans.

Even more impressive was China where the Ming dynasty ruled the wealthiest and most populous nation on earth, superbly self-confident in the superiority of its age-old civilization. The Mings sent the eunuch Cheng Ho on seven expeditions (1405-1433) which utterly dwarfed the voyages of Columbus. These expeditions, which typically included 27,000 men in fifty great ocean junks, ranged through Indonesia and visited India, Africa, the Red Sea and the Persian Gulf. Since little came of these voyages, only scholars remember Cheng Ho.

Since the days of the crusades Christendom had shrunk. Once flourishing Franciscan missions in the Middle East and even in China disappeared. Dramatically the voyages of Columbus and Vasco Da Gama reversed two centuries of contradiction and began the worldwide expansion of Christianity and European civilization. World War II ended the colonial era, but even today western ideas—science, technology, Marxism and modern nationalism—continue to transform society and culture in the developing nations.

The Spanish and Portuguese, fresh from the *Reconquista* and already spilling over into Africa, saw the missionary work in America and the Far East as part of their long struggle against Islam. Later they valued the missions as a chance to offset the loss of northern Europe to Protestantism. Although at times greedy and cruel, both Columbus and Cortes considered themselves as the instruments of divine providence for spreading the Gospel. The Christianization of the Indians, often only nominal, went ahead with amazing rapidity. One Franciscan wrote from Mexico in 1528: "Often we baptized in a single day 14,000 people, sometimes 10,000, sometimes 8,000." By 1548 Latin America had eighteen bishops. Unlike Columbus, many Europeans were interested only in exploiting the natives. When a priest urged the duty to spread the faith to the Indians, Francisco Pizzaro replied bluntly, "I have not come for any such reason. I have come to take away from them their gold." Although many explorers, merchants and administrators have given indispensible help to missionaries over the centuries, the greed and vice of old Christians, typified by Pizzaro, have been the greatest block to evangelization.

No missionary ever felt this tension more than Bartolomé de Las Casas (1474-1566), who owned an *encomienda* in Cuba. The *encomienda* was a grant of Indians to work their estates which the crown awarded to Spanish settlers on condition that they protect and evangelize their Indians, but in practice the *encomienda* system meant slavery and exploitation. In his Christmas sermon of 1511 a Dominican, Antonio Montesinos, denounced the Europeans for enslaving the Indians and working them to death. For three years this indictment festered in Las Casas; he then spoke out against the system, joined the Dominicans and devoted his life to seeking justice for the Indians. He returned to Spain several times to badger Charles V and Philip II into a more Christian policy. He was largely responsible for the New Laws of 1542 which drastically changed the *encomienda* system. Las Casas was not a man of moderation but an impassioned prophet. His *Very Brief Relation of the Destruction of the Indies*, which paints all Spaniards as power mad and all Indians as paragons of virtue, founded the concept of the noble savage and the "Black Legend" of Spanish cruelty. He was also less than fair in denouncing the missionary methods of the Franciscans. Yet his sincerity is unquestioned. He turned down the rich diocese of Cuzco and later accepted the poor see of Chiapas only at the insistence of Charles V. There he had to face down rioting mobs and the Inquisition itself in defending his work. He also put his own missionary methods into successful operation among the Indians of Guatemala.

Las Casas certainly did not convince all Spaniards of the injustice of their conquests, but he made the moral issues inescapably clear. Few colonial rulers have tried harder to protect the rights of native subjects than did Charles V and Philip II. Unfortunately colonial practice fell far short of Spanish law.

One way to prevent exploitation was to isolate the Indians from contact with creoles. The Jesuits tried to do this in their Paraguay reductions, which in fact spread far beyond the borders of modern Paraguay. The first reduction began in 1610, and within thirteen years there were twenty-three containing some 100,000 Indians. The reductions tried to Christianize the Indians and replace their semi-nomadic life with a stable economy based on farming and cattle raising. Each reduction consisted of a town containing up to 10,000

Indians with homes laid out in grid pattern. In the central plaza stood the church as the center of community life; usually there would be a school and special workshops as well. Life was happy and disciplined. The Indians produced handicrafts, religious art, even music, plays and a rudimentary Guarani literature. The Jesuits served not only as pastors but also as supervisors, agricultural experts, architects and diplomats with the outside world.

The jungle Utopia had its problems. At times the Indians grew nostalgic for the old ways and restive under discipline. Indian revolts cost the lives of at least five Jesuits. More serious, bands of Portuguese half-castes raided the reductions for slaves. The raids of 1628 killed, captured or dispersed 88,000 Indians. In desperation the Jesuits appealed to the Spanish crown for the right to arm the Indians. The Indian army repulsed the raiders, but then the Spanish government became fearful of a semi-independent state within a state. The Indians were disarmed and the raids began again; finally the government had to supply guns once more. There was also the internal problem of paternalism. The Jesuits failed to develop initiative and self-reliance among the Indians. They brought forward no Indians for ordination, and when the Spanish crown expelled the Jesuits in 1767, the Indians gradually dispersed, and the jungle won back the villages and choked the whitewashed baroque churches.

There was little Protestant missionary activity in the sixteenth and seventeenth centuries. Protestant leaders were preoccupied with establishing their communities in Europe. Some theologians were rather callous to missionary work; Johann Gerhard, for instance, claimed that Christ's command to preach to all nations applied only to the twelve apostles and was no longer binding on the church. In any event, Catholic Spain and Portugal had pre-empted the most promising mission fields. Only in the nineteenth century did large scale mission societies afford Protestantism an instrument for missionary activity at all comparable to the

Catholic religious orders. Nevertheless, Protestantism did produce an outstanding missionary in the Presbyterian John Eliot (1604-1690). As soon as he became pastor at Roxbury, Massachusetts, he started to study Pequot. A trickle of Indian converts began, but when Eliot recognized how hard it was for his converts to live as Christians in their native villages, he set up "Praying Towns" not unlike the Jesuit reductions. By 1671 there were fourteen such villages with some 3,600 Christian Indians. King Philip's War, which pitted the colonists against the pagan Indians, proved a severe but temporary setback. Eliot's greatest achievement was translating the Bible into the local Algonkian dialect. He also wrote catechisms and a grammar for the Indians. The enormous number and difficulty of Indian dialects hurt missionary work; all too often missionaries have tried to solve the problem by making the Indians learn Spanish or English and conform to the white man's culture. Eliot never yielded to that temptation.

Asia presented an even greater challenge to missionaries than America. Not only were the peoples more numerous, they possessed sophisticated cultural and religious traditions that were often older than those of Europe. There could be no question of sweeping away the old culture and replacing it with Christianity and European ways. The missionaries had to determine what traditions were compatible with Christianity and how the Gospel should be presented to fit the genius and mentality of the various Asian nations.

Among the first to recognize this problem clearly was St. Francis Xavier, one of Loyola's first companions in founding the Jesuits. Xavier sailed from Lisbon for India in 1541 as the first Jesuit missionary. The voyage to Goa, the nodal point of Portugal's network of commercial bases, took a year. For a century most missionaries to the Orient had to make the same harrowing voyage, on which a mortality rate of thirty percent was common enough. Xavier's ten years in the Orient were the greatest missionary career since St. Paul. For two years Xavier worked in India, mostly among the illiterate fisherfolk of Cape Comorin where he traveled from village to village reciting a few basic prayers in memorized Tamil.

Leaving new missionaries to carry on, he spent the next four years in Indonesia. In the Spice Islands he talked to merchants about China and questioned the convert Yajiro about his native Japan. The more he heard about the Japanese, the more he was fascinated. He returned to Goa to supervise the work of younger Jesuits fresh from Europe, then left for Japan.

Xavier landed at Kagoshima in August, 1549. He was the first missionary and the first westerner to penetrate the interior of the country. The Japanese, "the delight of my heart," more than fulfilled his expectations. Here was an open-minded people of great intelligence and industry; moreover there were few Portuguese merchants to disgrace the Gospel with their dissolute living. Xavier, the hidalgo, instantly understood the samurai code of honor so central to Japanese culture, but he made several serious mistakes: he expected a unified country and sought out the emperor for permission to preach Christ. In fact the emperor was a figurehead. Xavier quickly realized that the local daimyos, or feudal lords, would have to be won over piecemeal. Yajiro, his interpreter, incorporated several Buddhist concepts into the memorized sermons and prayers that Xavier used with his neophytes. Later the Jesuits gained a better understanding of Japanese and Buddhism and revised the misleading ideas. Cross-cultural translation of this kind raises perennial mission problems. When Xavier learned that the Japanese looked up to the Chinese as scholars and religious teachers, he recognized that a major mission success in China would advance the faith in Japan.

Xavier determined to enter China even though the Middle Kingdom had closed its borders to outside barbarians. His efforts to join an official embassy fell through. When his Portuguese friends dared not run the risk, Xavier paid a

Chinese merchant to smuggle him into China. On a little island off the China coast he died on December 3, 1552, waiting vainly for the merchant's junk.

Were Xavier an ordinary missionary, he could not escape the charges of wanderlust and adventurism, but he wore three hats when he went east. He was papal nuncio and a representative of King John III of Portugal; he was also the first Jesuit mission superior. As such he was the advanced scout of a growing army; by his death there were a dozen mission stations from Goa to Japan, and today seven thousand Jesuits serve the missions. Xavier's task was to map strategy for those who would follow.

Of Xavier's many projects Japan held the greatest promise. As he had recognized, the daimyos were the key to the situation. They could give or refuse permission to preach, and their conversion might lead to the conversion of their subjects. Twelve years after the first daimyo became a Christian in 1563 there were fifty thousand Christians in his territory. Japanese catechists, ranked in various grades, were the most effective apostles. By 1601 there were 250 of the highest grade, whose close association to the Jesuits included vows of celibacy and life-long service. That same year a bishop began ordaining the catechists. Meanwhile Franciscan and Dominicans had joined the Jesuits in Japan, not without friction. Altogether there were some 300,000 Japanese Christians.

Just when there seemed to be hope that Japan would become a Christian nation, two developments destroyed the Japanese church. By 1590 Hideyoshi had founded the Tokugawa shogunate and subjected all Japan to a single ruler for the first time in five hundred years. Hideyoshi then turned against the foreign religion. As early as 1587 he ordered the expulsion of the missionaries; twelve years later he crucified twenty-six Christians. His death the next year gave Christianity sixteen years of breathing space until his successors began the most intense persecution of the reformation era. There were 1,900 formal executions with every refinement of cruelty; many more died of imprisonment and harsh treatment. The persecution broke the back of the Japanese church. Japan closed her ports to all European traders except the Dutch, who were uninterested in making converts. Even so, isolated pockets of Christians were discovered by missionaries in the nineteenth century when Japan again opened her ports.

China at first seemed less accessible than Japan. A single emperor ruled China with the help of scholar-administrators trained in the Chinese classics. Jesuit plans aimed at finding a Chinese Constantine who would lead his nation to Christianity. Even if the emperor could not be converted, his good will would assure toleration. The spearhead of the Chinese mission must be an elite of priest-scholars who not only spoke Chinese but who had mastered enough of Chinese culture and literature to impress the emperor and the aristocracy and thereby open the country for widespread conversions. The westerners need not come empty-handed since western science and technology had already outstripped the Chinese in certain areas which the missionaries could use as an entree.

The Portuguese base of Macao was the obvious jump-off point; there the Italian Jesuit Matteo Ricci (1552-1610) studied Chinese and waited for an opportunity to enter China. In 1583 he succeeded in establishing himself at Shiuhing where he cultivated friendships with Chinese administrators. Dressed in the plum silk robes of a mandarin, Ricci managed to visit Peking in 1600 and present two clocks which fascinated the emperor. His ability to keep the clocks running and in repair established Ricci in the emperor's favor, but he also shared his western mathematics and geography with the Chinese. Ricci was a skilled map-maker who cultivated Chinese sensitivity by putting the Middle Kingdom in the center of his world maps. His studies proved for the first time that fabled medieval Cathay was in fact China.

Meanwhile Ricci built a nucleus church of four hundred in Peking. He wrote many books in Chinese on western science. More difficult was his task of translating Christian theology since Chinese had no equivalents for many basic Christian ideas. For God he had to use Lord of Heaven. What attitude should Christians take toward the worship of ancestors and Confucius? Ricci decided that properly understood these were civil customs and could be continued by Christians. Many later missionaries disagreed. Ricci also felt that Christian churches should be modelled on pagodas. In short, Christianity should adapt itself to Chinese culture as far as possible.

Ricci's death caused no serious setback because other Jesuits were trained to carry on his work; among them were the German astronomer Adam Schall and later the Flemish mathematician Ferdinand Verbiest. Even the Manchu conquest of China in the mid-seventeenth century failed to dislodge the Jesuits, who performed the same services for the Manchus as they had for the Mings. The great emperor K'ang Hsi studied mathematics with Verbiest.

In one sense Ricci's plan was a failure because no Chinese Constantine emerged, but without the imperial favor won by the scientists at Peking, no mission work would have been possible in a country as centralized and xenophobic as China. In almost all the provinces of eastern China Jesuits, Dominicans, Franciscans and others were making steady but unspectacular progress. Eleven bishops were appointed, one of whom was Chinese.

Their success might have been greater except for a bitter quarrel over Chinese rites. At issue was not liturgical language (Rome first granted, then rejected a Chinese liturgy), but ancestor worship and the whole larger question of adaptation. Nor was the problem restricted to China since some Jesuits in India had taken up Ricci's approach; indeed, missionaries will always face the problem of cultural adaptation. Many in China, including some Jesuits, felt Ricci had gone too far. After decades of controversy Rome sent out a legate, Tournon, who decided against the Chinese rites in 1707. Emperor K'ang Hsi, personally incensed, expelled many missionaries. Rome then offered some compromises but generally took a hard line on adaptation until the twentieth century.

The Philippines proved the greatest mission success in Asia. Spaniards coming from Mexico colonized the islands; the missionaries, who arrived in 1565, applied the methods of evangelization worked out in Latin America. As in Latin America they could count on government help. The primitive culture of the natives presented problems, to be sure, but these were easier than the difficulties encountered in the high cultures of Japan, China and India. The sixteenth century was also a great age of expansion for Islam, especially in India and Indonesia. Christianity coming from Spain via Mexico and Luzon faced Islam advancing northward from Indonesia. The two world religions met in Mindanao where even today Christian-Moslem tensions rack the great southern island of the Philippines.

The missionary surge of the sixteenth and early seventeenth centuries was the finest fruit of the Catholic reformation. The best missionaries of the era rival Christians of any age in their heroic service of God, but certain shortcomings limited their success. Although the Spanish and Portuguese kings gave valuable help to the early missionary thrust, their continued claim to control the church in mission lands hindered growth in the seventeenth and eighteenth centuries. Rome itself became increasingly rigid and unimaginative in adapting the Gospel to native conditions. Only rarely was the Bible translated into the native languages. There were only sporadic efforts to encourage native priests and nuns, to say nothing of bishops. Insistence on clerical celibacy was an obstacle, but the major factor which slowed the development of native clergy was European racism. A Latin liturgy made no sense in China and the Congo. Squabbles among the missionary orders wasted energy and scandalized non-believers. The sheer physical obstacles and primitive communications should not be underestimated. Sometimes it took missionaries ten years to get a reply to their letters. Thousands of missionaries died from disease, filth, bad water or wormy bread before reaching their stations. More often than not there were no adequate schools, grammars and dictionaries for learning native languages.

When the fervor of the Catholic reformation in Europe cooled, efforts abroad slowed. The enlightened eighteenth century abhorred nothing so much as enthusiasm, but without religious enthusiasm missionary work languishes. Toward the end of the century the missionaries suffered a series of crippling blows. In 1773 the Bourbon monarchs forced Clement XIV to suppress the Jesuits, who were the largest missionary order. The French Revolution and the decades of war and disorder that followed nearly destroyed many other religious orders and dried up the flow of missionaries. For Catholics almost as much as for Protestants the nineteenth century was a great age of new beginnings in mission lands.

Suggested Readings

Bainton, Roland. *Erasmus of Christendom*. New York, 1969.

Bainton, Roland. *Here I Stand: A Life of Martin Luther*. New York, 1950

Bangert, William V. *A History of the Jesuits*. St. Louis, 1972.

Dickens, Arthur G. *The Counter Reformation*. New York, 1969.

Dickens, Arthur G. *The English Reformation*. London, 1964.

Dunne, George. *A Generation of Giants*. Notre Dame, 1962.

Elliott, John H. *Imperial Spain, 1469-1716*. New York, 1964.

Evans, Joan, editor. *The Flowering of the Middle Ages*. New York, 1966.

Evennett, H. Outram. *The Spirit of the Counter-Reformation*. Cambridge, 1968.

Ferguson, Wallace K. *Europe in Transition, 1300-1520*. Boston, 1962.

Grimm, Harold J. *The Reformation Era, 1500-1650*. New York, 1973.

Hughes, Philip. *A History of the Church*, III. New York, 1947.

Jedin, Hubert. *A History of the Council of Trent*. St. Louis, 1957-1961.

Latourette, Kenneth Scott. *A History of the Expansion of Christianity*, III. Grand Rapids, 1970.

Knowles, David. *The Evolution of Medieval Thought*. Baltimore, 1962.

Knowles, David. *Christian Monasticism*. New York, 1969.

Knowles, David, with Dimitri Obolensky. *The Middle Ages.* New York, 1968.

Mattingly, Garrett. *The Armada.* Boston, 1957.

Neale, John E. *Queen Elizabeth.* New York, 1934.

O'Connell, Marvin. *The Counter-Reformation, 1559-1610.* New York, 1974.

Scarisbrick, J.J. *Henry VIII.* Berkeley, 1968.

Smith, Lacey Baldwin. *The Horizon Book of the Elizabethan World.* New York, 1967.

Southern, R.W. *Western Society and the Church in the Middle Ages.* Baltimore, 1970.

Spitz, Lewis W. *The Renaissance and Reformation Movements.* Chicago, 1971.

Trevor-Roper, Hugh, editor. *The Age of Expansion.* New York, 1968.

Wendel, Francois. *Calvin.* New York, 1963.

Wedgewood, Cecily V. *The Thrirty Years War.* London, 1938.